C000204775

foreword

In the 18th Century my ancestor, the Fourth Earl of Sandwich (1718-1792) invented a unique and convenient way to enjoy a healthy meal without having to leave the gaming table. Over 200 years later, the same spirit of innovation continues to inspire pioneering foodies like Phil Brown as they serve the public with a superb choice of wholesome lunchtime food, providing a welcome break in the busy working day for thousands of people. This little book is typical of Phil's style with its quirky morsels of sandwich trivia carefully selected and presented to please and delight. I am sure that you will find it the perfect accompaniment to a sandwich, and a useful gift for sandwich lovers everywhere.

John Sandwich

John Edward Hollister Montagu
11th Earl of Sandwich

The Sandwich Lovers Companion

Compiled by

Philip Brown

ISBN 978-0-9571957-7-6
(*International Sandwich Book Number*)
No.1

Designed and Produced by Plasma Media Ltd
Illustrated by Dai Owen

Published by Plasma Media Ltd - 2018

Contents

About the Author

Philip Brown founded Philpotts Quality Sandwiches in a 365 square foot premises at number 2 Goss Street, Chester in June, 1985. It was the first bespoke sandwich shop outside of London and is credited with being the first sandwich business in the world to put Coronation Chicken on its menu.

The name later contracted to PHILPOTTS as the business opened shops in Manchester, Shrewsbury, Edgbaston, Birmingham, Bristol, Liverpool and Leeds.

A succession of industry awards for its innovative and up market standard of offer and employee training gave the business 'blue ribbon' status and Philip sold out in 2006 with a turnover of £7.3 million and 194 employees. PHILPOTTS now totals 23 stores and is owned by Patisserie Valerie.

A lover of good food, Philip appeared on several TV programmes from Richard and Judy to Johnny Vaughan Tonight and Big Breakfast as well as a number of BBC TV food shows. He has been a frequent commentator on radio too.

Philip served on the management committee of the British Sandwich Association for more than ten years and became Chairman in 2002. In 2006 he was awarded the BSA Award for his long term contribution to furthering the sandwich industry. Philip is still innovating and has now opened the Sea Shanty Cafe in Trearddur Bay (Anglesey). With an interior as different as its food is good, this new beachside venture is enjoying restaurant success unparalleled for such a large premises in such a remote location.

Joshua Stevenson
Travel Journalist/Publisher

the

essential

Sandwich Companion

Disclaimer

The publisher wishes to point out that comments contained in this publication should be taken with a pinch of salt!

the A to Z of sandwiches

from Bap to Wrap

Arepa: Venezuela. A bun made from a fried
pan-cake like bread of ground corn or flour, water and
salt topped Dutch style with ingredients or containing
(folded around) meat, tomatoes, shrimps or other fish,
salad, cheese or egg. Often served hot, the Arepa can
be griddled or contact grilled. While originating from
Venezuela, Arepa are now popular in most South and
Central American countries.

Bad Sandwich (1) : Obviously a sandwich made with
yesterday's bread or ingredients that are sparse or do
not fill the corners and edges, possibly containing
cartilage/bone/gristle or some other horrid and
unexpected interruption to the enjoyment of the
sandwich.

"Bad Sandwich"(2): Industry equivalent of "A difficult
serve", an unexpected equipment failure or mishap,
an idea that has gone wrong, a negative outcome.

Bagel: A hard ring or doughnut shaped bread bun made from boiled dough without yeast and characteristic of Jewish baking. Tough texture, but improves dramatically with toasting.

Baguette: French style single portion crusty long slim loaf, which has migrated successfully to the UK and now virtually the rest of the world.

Bait Box: Bait Bag. North England (Lancashire. Yorkshire, Cumbria, Durham). Colloquial for a sandwich or packed lunch container. Contents referred to as bait.

Banjo Sandwich: A sandwich which sheds crumbs or ingredients which land on your shirt front necessitating several up and down movements of the right hand to brush things off. The action looks as if one is playing an invisible banjo.

Banh Mi. First seen in San Francisco and New York, this is essentially a Vietnamese sandwich. Made in a French Baguette it contains virtually any meat at all mixed half and half with pickled vegetables and onion. Firmly in the category of 'street food' Banh Mi can now be seen in restaurants and market stalls in London.

Bap: Unsophisticated soft round white roll usually 'filled' with ham, cheese or egg. 'Filled' is a misnomer on this occasion because baps tend to inhabit the lower end of the market where price dictates mean portions as well as poor quality ingredients.

Barm: Barm cake, Lancashire. Another word for Bap but flatter than the latter and, in sandwich terms, carrying the same shortcomings.

Batch or Batch cake: Thick crusted, soft centred round bread rolls baked close to each other so that when pulled apart they have white crumby sides. Offered for sale in the same way as Bap and Barm, but slightly larger and a better eat.

Baton: Another name for a French Stick. So named because it looks like something you could hit somebody over the head with or indeed pass on to the next runner during a relay race.

Battery Sandwich: Expression coined by Keith Waterhouse writing in SAGA magazine to describe factory made sandwiches. The alternative being "A buxom lady in a pinny with a cottage loaf, a slab of butter and a bread knife".

BBT: Brie, Bacon and Tomato sandwich.

Beer and Sandwiches: Legendary 60s Entree to wage negotiations between Government Ministers and Trade Union officials.

Binlid: Liverpool. A very large flat batch or barm cake popular option at one time in Liverpool sandwich bars. "D'you wannit on bread or a binlid".

Bisin: A naturally occurring agent capable, so it is claimed by its discoverers, of destroying the bacteria that cause meat, fish, eggs and dairy products to rot. Scientists working at the University of Minnesota claim the technology could extend the life of sandwiches for months even years. The writer is sceptical. (See this chapter 'Curling':)

BLT: Bacon, Lettuce and Tomato, one of the most ingenious combinations of ingredients for a sandwich. Originated in the USA possibly as far back as the 1950s.

BLOAT: Bacon, Lettuce, Onion, Avocado, Tomato sandwich. Source unknown.

Battery Sandwich: Expression coined by Keith Waterhouse to describe factory made sandwiches.

Bloomer: Extended or 'stretched' domed 'cob' (See this chapter 'Cob':) usually white, notably crusty and viable for sandwich making in so far as it can be cut into numerous slices of equal size. The cob has the flavour and the crust but is circular so that no more than two slices are likely to be the same size.

Brioche: Very light eating bread made with egg. Popular in a roll form more often in restaurant situations rather than sandwich bars. Used by the restaurant Lobster Burger to create lobster sandwiches if a customer doesn't want to do battle with a lobster in its shell. At the time of writing one of these sandwiches costs the customer £20.00

Bread Sandwich (1): Two slices of bread with a slice of bread in between. (See chapter 'Sandwiches on Stage':)

Bread Sandwich (2): Experienced by the writer aboard an Indian Airways (domestic) flight from Jaipur to Udaipur in 2003. The interesting dark material between two slices of white bread (without crusts) turned out to be a slice of brown bread buttered both sides.

Brechdan: Welsh for sandwich. Brechdannau: sandwiches. Literally 'slices of bread'.

British Rail Sandwich: National focus of post-war derision which was probably responsible for damning sandwiches in the public mind for 50 years.

Broodje: Dutch for sandwich. from Brood, Dutch for Bread.

BSA: British Sandwich Association. Trade association based at Association House, 18C Moor Street, Chepstow, NP165DB. With membership comprising mainly of sandwich manufacturers, suppliers, multiple retailers and supermarkets, producers, packagers and equipment makers, it has done much to focus the industry and promote higher standards. Acting as a voice for the industry, it has made effective representations to government on issues such as labelling, food safety and VAT. With somewhere under 50 sandwich bar members out of a possible 16,000, it cannot yet claim to speak for the industry as a whole. Director Jim Winship (See this chapter 'Jim Winship':)

Bulkie: Jewish. Cholla Bread (sweeter than ordinary bread and traditionally eaten on Friday nights) made into a plait (See this chapter 'plait:)' or a roll with a scrolled top crust.

Butty: Fond North of England term for a sandwich. Most common in Liverpool.

Butt-head: Term applied to one who eats, sleeps and breathes sandwiches. Source unknown.

Burrito: This is like a large and fat wrap. Often 'made to order' in front of the customer, typical ingredients are, as the name suggests, from Mexican cuisine: chilli beef, chopped olives, chicken, cheese, sour cream, chopped lettuce. Containing a much larger volume of ingredients than its wrap or pita brothers (or sisters*) the Burrito is often wrapped entirely in foil at point of sale . This enables the eater to expose one end and start eating without everything dropping out. * Arguments continue over what sex a sandwich is. Perhaps the French, who sex everything in their language, have given us the answer. (See this chapter 'Le Sandwich Anglaise':)

Cape Sandwich: Situated in the Rockingham Bay area of Queensland, Australia, it was named after the Fourth Earl of Sandwich by Captain James Cook during his first voyage of discovery (1768 to 1771) aboard Endeavour. Sandwich did not feature greatly in Cook's life at this time since he only named one cape after him but clearly, he (Sandwich) had, as Postmaster General in Grantham's government, been helpful. After this voyage, the Earl became a great admirer of Cook and a 'fast' friend of Joseph Banks to whom he offered a place on Cook's second voyage (Resolution). Later, after 1771, as First Lord of the Admiralty, he gave generous help to Cook in his official capacity, and was a major sponsor of his Third and final voyage. Cape Sandwich is the north eastern extremity of what became Hinchinbrook Island, the name of Sandwich's Huntingdonshire home.

Carry out: Meal made at home and taken to work. Most often comprising of sandwiches.

Ceapaire: Gaelic for food enclosed in bread. An Irish Sandwich.

Cheese and Onion: Still the writer's favourite sandwich. Cheese must be Cheddar, mature and strong. Onion must be white and raw. Mayonnaise must be Hellmann's and in plenty. Bread must be thumb print fresh and white. Washed down with an ambient pint of full cream milk.

Cheese topped Baton: Same as a Baton but with cheese melted over the crust. The cheese gives nothing good to the bread in my view. It tends to prevent the top crust baking and usually being low grade cheese, doesn't have any flavour. The cheese also has a drying effect on bread when baked together. Mixing novel ingredients with bread making doe can be exciting, particularly with the use of nuts and herbs, but the drying effect cuts in again with tomato.

Chicken Abdication: (See this chapter 'Chicken Coronation':). A chicken sandwich (Coronation or otherwise) which presents an inadequate quantity of chicken, even none at all, to its hungry consumer. This situation can come about when the sandwich maker dices the chicken too finely and bulks the mixture out with excessive mayonnaise and/or other bulking agents so as to reduce the chicken content at a molecular level, possibly unintentionally, to an unacceptably small number of parts per million.

Chocolate Sandwich: Sexual encounter involving two white ladies and one black gentleman made famous in Lindsay Anderson's film 'O Lucky man' (1973) starring Malcolm Mc Dowell and Arthur Lowe.

Chorleywood: The Chorleywood bread process (CBP) was developed in 1961 by the British Baking Industries Research Association based in Chorleywood. By 2009 this process was being used to make 80% of UK bread. What we know as "supermarket bread". Compared to the older bulk fermentation process, CBP is able to use lower protein wheat and produce bread in a shorter time. This enabled the mass production of sandwiches and marked a milestone in the bakery/sandwich industry.

Ciabatta: Italian bread rolls made in such a way as to have large cavities inside. Made with sourdough and olive oil. Very popular in sandwich bars, restaurants and delicatessens.

Clam sandwich: USA. Romantic term adopted as the name for a Californian company making kiteboards, skateboards and surfboards.

Clapping: Sandwich manufacturing term. The act of closing two halves of a cut sandwich together to make it ready for insertion in a triangular packet.

Club Sandwich: Having three or more slices of bread and two or more layers each of different ingredients. In UK and USA generally containing white turkey or chicken meat on one strata with bacon or cheese or both in the other. In New Zealand, the sandwich is made specifically without crusts.

Cob: Large circular domed loaf of bread.

Colin's Sandwich: Wistful 1980s TV sit-com starring Mel Smith as a British Rail booking clerk with writing ambitions.

Companage: Food eaten with bread.

Conewich: Forlorn commercial attempt in 2000 to re-shape the sandwich from its familiar format into a cone. Packaged in a crushproof plastic sundae container (conetainer?) it was a sandwich manufacturer's dream invention because it allowed perfectly portioned ingredients to be easily delivered by machine into the wide end of the cone. The designers sadly forgot to think about the consumer who, already struggling with 'pyramiding' (See this chapter) were now faced with ingredient overwhelm at one end and deficit at the other. An inherently flawed idea that failed to catch on.

Beer and Sandwiches: Legendary 60s Entrée to wage negotiations.

"Just heard... pasties are coming out in support"

Conney-onney: Liverpool. Sandwich made with Nestles Condensed Milk. Credited with generating a state of euphoric happiness, particularly amongst children during World War II. Still popular up to the 1970s, long after the end of the rationing and sugar shortages that first took the excitement of this creation to stratospheric heights.

Current Bun: More often these days called a tea cake. Bread bap with a sweet glazed top and currents baked into the dough. Also cockney rhyming slang for Son or Sun or One. Also "Who is your currant bun?" meaning "Who is your latest girl friend ?".

Cradle: Substantial sandwich box resembling a baby's cradle but enclosed and having hooks either end. Used by miners to suspend lunch from a horizontal wire slung along the roof of a currently worked lead to keep it out of the water. Tea or lunch break often referred to as 'cradle time'.

Criticism Sandwich: Managerial technique whereby an employee receives criticism preceded and followed by praise to counter possible feelings of low worth.

Croissant: Flaky bread roll made of yeast dough similar to puff pastry. Light in texture and appearance but high in butter fat. French origin and so called because of its 'crescent' shape. Sandwich ingredients are usually grilled cheese with or without bacon, or mushrooms in white sauce.

Croque-monsieur: French origin but common parlance in most of Europe. Ham and cheese open sandwich fried in butter or grilled.

Crust of Bread: Crust being the top and ends of a 'tin' loaf of bread or the higher baked top of any bap/barm/roll/cob/bloomer etc etc etc. Also used in Cockney rhyming slang to mean Head, hence "Use yer Crust" but more commonly "Use yer Loaf".

Cubano: Cuban sandwich. Local bread usually containing ham and roasted pork (suckling pig is almost the national dish of Cuba) which has been marinated in a sauce made of garlic, pepper, oregano lemon juice and salt and known as mojo. These days the sandwich can be toasted on a contact grill or toastie press and contains an ever-widening assortment of ingredients. Variations include use of different cheeses and the addition (particularly in Belgium) of béchamel sauce. The bread is always white. In Cuba itself, the Cubano is quite scarce since there are no sandwich shops though sandwiches are occasionally sold out of ground floor windows.

Croque-madame: Croque-monsieur with a fried egg on top.

Curling: Something that happens to old sandwiches. Exposed to the open air for an extensive period of time, the effect is caused by the top surface of the top slice of bread drying and contracting to cause a stress differential with its underside. Common during the last century when sandwiches were frequently made of poor quality bread and displayed for hours in ambient conditions. Thankfully, rarely seen today due to modern food storage and display practices.

Cut: Generally, to part or sever something with a sharp blade or pair of scissors. Sometimes an alternative to 'canal'. In sandwich terms this word has come to mean "make". See this chapter "Freshly cut sandwiches" attempting to mean "recently made". Once heard from a mother disparaging a daughter's poor career choice and seeing the enormous growth of take-out food "Ooh you should 'av gone cuttin' sandwiches ".

Cutter: Barbados. Deep fried flying fish sandwich. A Bajan Salt bread roll (which in spite of its name isn't really salty at all) with a fried flying fish inserted. Other fried fish steaks are also common, tuna, marlin or local Billfish. These days, as with so many other forms of hand held bread snack, the choice of ingredients has broadened to include ham, fried egg etc etc.

Doorstep: Fond term for a thick sandwich, having the appearance of a doorstep due to generous hand cut slices of bread. Caterers for the 'working classes' tended to provide a satisfying meal by enlarging the bread content, keeping the expensive ingredient element to a minimum.

Double Decking: The habit of placing two sandwiches on top of each other and eating them together. Useful technique for the hungry at weddings and funerals where sandwiches tend to be thin and few.

Earl of Sandwich: Trading name adopted by Orlando Montagu, second son of John Montagu, Eleventh Earl of Sandwich (See 'Foreword), for his sandwich business venture which commenced trading from a railway arch in Hackney in 2001. Featured on BBC's 'Trouble at the Top' in February 2002, the business had a rocky start but determination from the founder and sound business advice prevailed. While the original concept (very high-end sandwiches delivered to offices in the city of London in Landrovers) was abandoned, the name has been attached to a chain of sandwich bars in the USA. This succeeded in bringing the Sandwich family back into sandwiches after a break of just 239 years.

Enchilada: Flour tortilla fried in hot fat with meat rolled up inside and seasoned with chilli sauce. Mexican dish popular throughout the Americas, a sort of forerunner to the Rolly. (See this chapter 'Rolly':)

ESA: European Sandwich makers Association. Based at BSA headquarters in Oxfordshire. (See 'BSA':)

Falafel: Through and through this is a Middle Eastern snack. The falafel itself is a fried ball of modestly spiced chickpeas. However, stuffed inside a pita bread and slathered in tahini with lettuce, cucumber and onions, it merits a mention in this book.

Curling: Something that happens to old sandwiches.

Fast Food Chain: ....Notoriously competitive ....

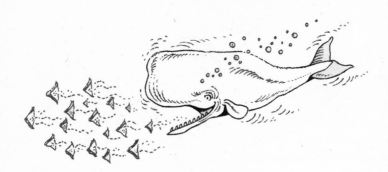

Fast Food Chain: Any branded take away food offer with more than two retail outlets. Giant combines with 100s or 1000s of outlets are notoriously competitive in their fight for market share.

Filling: Common term referring to the ingredients of a sandwich. Poor imagery in the writer's view, being associated with dentistry and generally not something one wants in ones mouth.

Finger Sandwiches: A sandwich with the crusts cut off and then cut into four long "fingers". These generally form part of a high end 'Afternoon Tea' with cakes, scones and Cornish cream. 'Fingering' makes sandwiches very easy to eat and the losing of crusts is a particular treat. It is also fair to say that eating finger sandwiches is considerably more decorous than chomping into the average wedge. Old people perhaps with few teeth or dentures can also eat finger sandwiches more easily.

Flatbread: This is not unlike a naan in appearance but comprises a fluffier wheat based doe which can be doubled over to hold ingredients as with a 'Pocket sandwich'. (See this chapter 'Pocket sandwich:')

Food to Go: Modern term for what used to be called a snack or take away food. Food to Go (probably soon to be shortened to FTG) now covers any kind of food at all that the vendor or purchaser wishes to be eaten elsewhere. In reality, Food to Go means "Ready to eat but not here." More and more food is eaten literally walking down the street. Embraces street food and includes sandwiches.

Food on the move: Trade show covering equipment and trends for the above.

French: Generic term for almost any long slim roll or baguette eg "Ham and Swiss on French please". French Kiss: Mischievous term for a tongue sandwich.

Freshly Cut Sandwiches: Sandwiches which, however old they may be, have recently been cut. (The word cut is here used to mean "made" but not everyone knows that). The adverb 'freshly' can only apply to the verb 'cut', but not the sandwiches.

Fresh Cut Sandwiches: Confusing words often seen chalked on boards beside caravans in lay-bys on busy main roads, attached to farm gates or outside small shops.

Food on the move: Street Food:
" ..the new name for fast food.."

Fresh Cut-Sandwiches: A quantity of recently made sandwiches which have also been cut.

Gavrilo Princip: The man who shot Archduke Franz Ferdinand in 1914 and, consequently started WW1. The story goes that he was eating a sandwich immediately before his successful assassination bid. For full details (See chapter 'Sandwiches at War':)

Gerald Ratner: The man who 'gave the lie' to the expression "there is no such thing as bad publicity". His thriving jewellery business collapsed following an unfortunate remark comparing his product to a sandwich during a speech to the Institute of Directors in April 1991. He said: "We even sell a pair of earrings for under a pound, which is cheaper than a prawn sandwich from Marks & Spencer's. But I have to say the earrings probably won't last as long." Ratner's went into swift decline from which it never recovered.

Giant Rolly: Popular offer sporadically available from Harrod's food Halls and at one time from PHILPOTTS. (See this chapter 'Rolly':)

Goblin caves: Sandwich manufacturers term for the small gaps that can occur within the curves of lettuce leaves, particularly iceberg, which create air pockets. In the writers view, a handmade sandwich is better and more nutritious if made with a 'flat' lettuce. To a sandwich manufacturer, Iceberg may be more convenient having a longer shelf life than a 'flat', and it may introduce 'crunch' to the sandwich, while also being an inexpensive bulking agent, but it also introduces water which in our view, negates all the other considerations. A strong green flat lettuce such as Webs Wonderful gives more flavour and better nutrition. Otherwise rather than being a manufacturers nuisance, pockets of air (Goblin caves) add flavour and texture to a handmade product.

Gratia Placendi: Italian. "The delight of pleasing". Once used by well known sandwich chain PHILPOTTS in an advertisement designed to stimulate the curious.

Greencore: Formerly a firm which morphed out of Irelands state owned sugar beet industry. Now probably the largest sandwich manufacturing business in the world.

Intense Tomato: Name given to a new breed of plum tomato developed by Raynor Foods of Chelmsford in 2010. It has thicker cell walls and helps retain moisture thus eliminating the risk of soggy sandwiches.

Hamburger: Ball of ground meat, usually beef, bound with egg and seasoning then squashed into a circular patty and cooked. Often eaten between the top and bottom pieces of a sliced bun, it is sometimes mistakenly called a sandwich. Style originated in Hamburg, Germany, and was taken by migrants to the USA from where it has been re-exported around the world.

Hawaii: Name given to the Sandwich Islands when they passed from British to American ownership in 1898, later to become the 50th US state in 1959.

Hoagie, hero, sub, grinder, spukie: These all describe the same kind of sandwich but are peculiar to different areas of the USA. Ingredients are almost always meats of some kind stacked thickly into a long 'French' roll.

Fresh Cut Sandwiches : Confusing words...

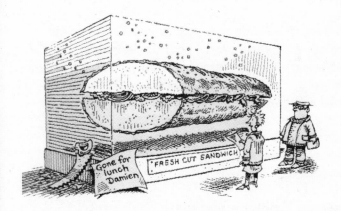

Hold: USA. No. Becoming common parlance in the UK and other English-speaking countries. Shortened from "withhold" or " I want no (mayonnaise) meaning "do not apply this ingredient (to my sandwich)..." "hold the mayo.", " Hold the onions ", ketchup etc. etc. English translation: "Would you be so kind as to not add any mayonnaise (say) to my sandwich".

Hot dog: Universally accepted name for what was originally a sausage sandwich. Popularised in the USA, it generally takes the form of a warm Frankfurter style sausage placed in a bread roll of similar length and served with fried onions and mustard or tomato ketchup. Synonymous with fairgrounds and mobile vendors, they are poor quality food but tempting in the extreme and quite enjoyable for the hungry or intoxicated.

Imaginary Sandwich Bar: Alexei Sayle's comic vehicle for the acclaimed performer/writer Alexei Sayle to deliver entertainment and philosophy to radio audiences. EG, what can sandwiches tell us about history? He doubts the Earl of Sandwich was the first person to put a bit of meat between two slices of bread (as does the writer) and hypothesises that before the Earls brainwave, if people wanted a snack they had to squeeze a football between two bricks, or place a dog between two bigger dogs.

He also casts doubt upon the naming of other new ideas from aristocratic inventors like the Marquis of Hovercraft and the Duke of Catflap.

In or Out?: UK. The question by which a server determines the tax status and level of service to offer a customer buying food in a sandwich bar situation. Food consumed on the premises attracts VAT (Value Added Tax) while the same food taken away does not.

ISA: International Sandwich Association. Based at the same address as the BSA (See this chapter BSA:) Director Jim Winship. (See this chapter 'Jim Winship':)

Jambon-beurres: France, Ham sandwiches. Since the late 19th century, France's most popular take away hand held bread snack until overtaken by Le Hamburger in 2017. In that year 1.46 billion hamburgers outsold 1.22 billion of the above.

Jam Butty: White bread raspberry jam sandwich. Popular post World War II treat fondly remembered mainly in the North. Also colloquial for British police cars in the 60s and 70s when cream colouring with a bright red horizontal stripe along each side was the contemporary livery.

Jim Winship: Founding Director of the BSA and ISA (see this chapter) and responsible as such for lubricating growth in the sandwich industry.

Katz Deli: Famous New York deli specialising in cured meat sandwiches. Specifically, Pastrami on Rye. See chapter 'Famous Sandwiches'. Used as a film location several times. Displays a hanging ovular sign from the ceiling saying "Send a salami to your boy in the army".

Kiwi Takeaway: Sanger from New Zealand. (See this chapter 'Sanger':)

Kiri Te Kanawa: Singer from New Zealand.

Kidney-punch: Cockney rhyming slang for 'Lunch'. As in "See yer in the rubbadub (pub) for a spot of kidney punch."

Knuckle Sandwich: UK colloquialism for a punch in the mouth.

Liver Sandwich: Early 20th century cure for anaemia. Raw liver sandwiches were considered a cure or tonic for sufferers of anaemia. The bread was probably simply a vehicle to protect the consumer from the sight and smell, not to mention the unpalatable texture they were about to ingest.

Le Hamburger: Recently reported (March 2018) to have dethroned the French jambon baguette as the most popular take-out food in France. The rise of the burger is attributed to it becoming a restaurant menu item sold with full table service. Only 30% of hamburgers sold in France are bought in fast food outlets. Source: - Food consultancy Gira Conseil who conducted the research.

Le Sandwich Anglaise: Claimed by Sandwich and Snack News (see this chapter 'Sandwich and Snack News') (sandwich industry organ) to have "taken snacking to new heights" in parts of Europe where this term has become common parlance for the wedge. (See this chapter 'Wedge':)

Loaf of Bread: Cockney rhyming slang for 'Head' as in "Use yer Loaf". Also essential for sandwich making.

Lomita: A speciality of the Moo Grill in London's Cobb Street, the Lomita originates in Argentina.
A characterful ovular bread roll is stuffed with beef such as only Argentina can produce. As usual, the menu has widened to include salads, ham, cheese and fried eggs with a generous dollop of chimichurri sauce.

Lox: (1) Sandwich recipe of finely chopped smoked salmon mixed with cream cheese. Popular breakfast fare in New York served in a bagel. EG "Gimme a larx (larks's) bagel".

Lox: (2) A particular type of preserved salmon.

Lox: (3) Act of loading liquid oxygen fuel into a spacecraft.

Mcdonalds: A global hamburger chain. Considered an arm of US imperialism in many countries. Outlets in France were frequently attacked by protesters 20 years ago. Yet France is now McDonalds most profitable market outside the US with 1,400 restaurants. "McDo" as the French call it, offers McCamembert and McBaguette burgers as well as beer. In the 1990's McDonalds tried to re brand their product as a sandwich to ride the tide of growing popularity that sandwiches were enjoying. However efforts by the BSA (see this chapter BSA) halted this by publishing the 'correct' definition of a sandwich, crucially a "cold assembled "product. (See this chapter 'Sandwich':)

Mayonnaise: In the writer's view, an essential ingredient for most sandwiches. Made of olive oil and egg yolk blended together into a thick pale mixture, mayonnaise can enhance fish, cheese, salad, chicken, ham and of course egg. Often simply referred to as "Mayo" it is quite different to Salad Cream which has a much sharper taste and is a much lower end of the market ingredient. Having said this, salad cream does have its place in certain sandwich situations.

Minefield: Sandwich containing a powerful surprise ingredient deposited in such a way that the consumer is unaware of which mouthful will "blow his or her mouth off". Fresh English mustard or fresh horseradish sauce are favourites but a pleasing effect can be achieved with soft green peppercorns or a generous concealed dollop of strong chilli sauce, a jalapeno or even a small piece of raw chilli. Author's favourite. Fresh Mint and Mature cheddar Mustard Minefield. Create a solid layer of fresh mint leaves over the cheese after applying three random mines. Spin the sandwich several times before cutting so that you (or the customer) will not know where or when the mystery taste explosion will occur.

Mrs Beeton's Sandwich: An elaborate collection of recipes from the nineteenth century, published in her famous Book of Household Management. With exotic and mysterious names such as "Clent", "Princess", "Pompadour", "Spanish", "Sefton", etc. Most recipes required the ingredient to be "rubbed through a fine sieve" before being put between two slices of thin bread and "pressed well", "trimmed", "cut into desired shapes" and most importantly, "dished daintily". It is worth remembering that the readership of Mrs Beeton's book were more often making food for people with poor, painful, wooden or no teeth at all. Her description of Rolled Sandwiches (See this chapter 'Rolled sandwich':) suggests that the nineteenth century definition of a sandwich included absolutely any form of hand held bread snack.

Muff: Short for Muffin, a type of round barm similar to a Binlid (See this chapter Binlid:) but popular in Manchester in the 80's. Particularly familiar to customers of Melia's sandwich bar in John Dalton Street where front of house staff would shriek to the kitchen "BLT on a brown muff" eg.

Muffulata: (Muffuletta) Sandwich associated with New Orleans. Olive salad with mortadella and provolone cheese. The word Muffulata however refers to the traditional Sicilian sesame seed covered round bun which purists require to be used for this sandwich. Other ingredients include minced garlic and Italian chopped ham.

Naanwich: Pocket sandwich or flatbread made with Indian Naan bread.(See this chapter 'Pocket sandwich':)

One Sandwich Short of a Picnic: UK: A person having only nineteen shillings in the pound. USA: a 'deli pickle'.

Open Sandwich: Two slices of bread on a plate side by side with ingredients placed on both. Requiring a deft stroke to close both sides together without spilling the ingredients. The gimmick is impractical and impossible when the offer sometimes contains only one piece of bread. Popular in Holland, the 'open' element probably developed from the vendor's desire to show off the otherwise hidden ingredients. Those ingredients have themselves outmatched the bread and have sometimes even acquired a portion of chips or crisps alongside, making the whole affair something to be eaten with a knife and fork.

It is unfair, for this reason to call this form of food a sandwich. If a sandwich is something that is hand held, then the Dutch Open sandwich does NOT qualify. Ploughman's lunch would be more appropriate.

Outsandwiched: Expression coined by Peter Bartlett, while Managing Director of Breadwinners sandwich manufacturing company, for their advertising slogan "Never knowingly outsandwiched". Derived from John Lewis's "Never knowingly undersold".

Palegg: A Scandinavian word meaning practically anything at all that can be put into a sandwich.

Panini: Stumpy cigar shaped roll (French) loaded with ingredients and then clamped between the two hot surfaces of a fluted contact grill until heated throughout, flattened and toasted.

Pastrami: Type of Cured beef, not unlike salt beef, highly seasoned and smoked. Popular in Yiddish culture served on Rye bread with a pickled dill cucumber and mustard. (See Chapter 'Famous Sandwiches':)

Peanut Butter and Jelly Sandwich: With 'pumpkin pie' and 'grits', the peanut butter and jelly (jam) sandwich seems to have become an important part of 'down home' American culinary culture, spoken of with pride by US citizens while elsewhere generally ignored.

Pecyn Bwyd: Welsh. Container in which sandwiches are taken to work. Also 'Bocs bwyd' and 'Tin bwyd' (particularly mining) borrowing 'bocs' and 'tin' from the English while 'bwyd' simply means 'food'.

Peppered Brioche: Brioche roll with ground black pepper added to the dough prior to baking. Unusual and found in restaurant situations more than sandwich bars. Last observed in the Sea Shanty Café at Trearddur Bay (Anglesey) with piri piri chicken and melted cheddar ingredients.

Philpotts: Blue Ribbon bespoke sandwich shop chain founded in 1985 by the author. Res ipsa loquitur. (See this chapter 'Res ipsa loquitur':)

Piece: Scotland. Dundonian term used extensively in Perthshire and other parts of Eastern Scotland to mean packed sandwiches or other food to be eaten at 'Piece time' (lunch or tea break). Shortened to 'piece' from piece of bread, cheese, cake etc.

Pierre-Jean Grosley: 18th century French travel writer who first described the story of the 4th Earl of Sandwich asking for beef between two slices of toasted bread. The story is much loved by sandwich marketeers and while it may describe the naming of this kind of food, it does not explain the origin of it. A truer picture can be found in this book. (See chapter The History of Sandwiches:)

Piroshki or Pirozki: Russian and East European rich yeasted bread roll with diced cooked bacon fat (like Italian Prosciuto) baked into it. Eaten with sandwich ingredients or more often just on its own.

Plait: Bread roll with a twisted crust plaited from one end to the other. Pleasant when fresh because it delivers more 'crust' than a plain roll.

Platter: Universal appellation for a tray or 'plate' of sandwiches. The provision of sandwich platters to offices enables sandwich shops to extend their window of sales opportunity beyond the brief lunchtime period. Trays made of aluminium foil, china, plastic and even basket are used but all are referred to as platters.

Po'Boy: Shortened from "Poor Boy" this is a Louisiana sandwich served on a baguette containing oysters, shrimps or catfish with a variety of sauces or just lemon juice and mayonnaise. The range has of course expanded to now include Beef, turkey or ham which, in line with the industry, become ever more popular.

Pocket Sandwich: Hand held bread snack made with one slice of bread (or a bread pocket) folded around the ingredients. The 'carrier' can also be an entire small loaf with the insides pulled out and discarded, or pita bread, tortilla, flatbread or even pizza bread/dough in which case, when heated, it becomes a Calzone. If the pizza bread carrier is square and rolls the ingredients into a log, this then become a Stromboli.

Pret a Manger: Ready made sandwich retail chain which enjoyed meteoric growth in 1990s London. The founders Julian Metcalf and Sinclaire Beecham were decorated with honours (MBEs) for "services to catering". The group was partially sold to McDonalds and is currently expanding to the USA and other UK cities outside London. An attempt to take the chain to Hong Kong in the 1990's was an expensive failure.

Pyramiding: A sandwich makers careless habit of piling ingredients into the centre of a piece of bread and failing to spread to the edges and corners thus leaving those two areas all but empty. If the sandwich is subsequently quartered, the eater now has one corner jammed full of ingredient with insufficient bread, and the other two corners not only proffering crusts but hardly any ingredient either. See Chapter 'Secrets of Super Sandwich Making'.

Quesadilla: Flour or corn tortilla which is filled with cheese and then grilled. Other items, such as a savoury mince mixture of spices or vegetables, are often added, then they are cooked on a griddle. A full quesadilla involves two tortillas filled with cheese and stacked on top of each other. Halves are a single tortilla filled with cheese and folded into a half-moon shape. (See this chapter Pocket sandwich:)

RCP: Reverse Crust Profiling. The technique by which bread from an irregular shaped loaf can be matched to form a sandwich without overlaps. This is achieved by buttering and using the reverse side of alternate slices.

Res Ipsa Loquitur: Latin. "Which speaks for itself". Used in law and sometimes sandwiches. (See this chapter PHILPOTTS:)

Pyramiding: Habit of piling ingredients...

"Whadya mean Pharoah doesn't like salad?"

Reuben: See chapter 'Famous Sandwiches'.

Roll: Sausage shaped small individual loaf so named because the dough is 'rolled' before baking. Small establishments may offer 'filled rolls' being ready made up sandwiches using this bread while smaller versions ('bridge' and 'finger' rolls) are, or were popular at children's' parties, cut horizontally and spread with egg or meat paste. Happy days!

Rolled Sandwich: Also known in France as 'Tartine Roulees'. Mrs Beeton is very specific, here reproduced. "Ingredients: six ounces of finely chopped cooked chicken, 2 ounces of finely chopped ham or tongue, two tablespoonfuls of mayonnaise sauce, brown bread.
Method: Pound the chicken and ham (or tongue) in a mortar until smooth, adding a little liquid butter to facilitate the process. Season to taste and rub through a fine sieve, then stir in the mayonnaise sauce. Cut some thin slices of bread and butter, trim off the crusts, spread them with this preparation, roll up firmly, wrap them lightly in a clean cloth and let them remain in a cool place for one hour. Dish them daintily on a folded serviette or a lace paper and serve garnished with small cress."

Rolly: Flour tortilla or similar with ingredients rolled inside. Differing from a wrap in so far as the ends have not been folded towards the middle to create a parcel.

Roti: When Indian labourers arrived in Trinidad they brought their cooking techniques and flavours with them. The roti is a flat bread wrapped around spiced meats and vegetables. Popular now not just in the West Indies but most other developed city centres.

Round: One complete sandwich, i.e. having two whole slices of bread. 'A round of sandwiches' is confusingly plural but still refers to one sandwich, although it may have been cut into two or four. It has been argued that since a round of toast is one slice of bread toasted, the expression is incorrect. However, the marrying of two slices of bread with a layer of ingredients in between binds both slices into a single entity, though square in shape, or two triangles (or rectangles) - one round.

RTA: Not Roast beef, Tomato and Avocado as the name might suggest. The initials here reflect the appearance of the sandwich rather than the ingredients. The RTA is made with corned beef and cream cheese with copious amounts of tomato ketchup. It does indeed resemble something from a particularly nasty Road Traffic Accident.

RTG: 'Ready to Go' being a made up sandwich packaged for immediate sale and removal from the premises. This sandwich is for the man or woman in a hurry. A 'Made to Order' bespoke sandwich may also be sold for taking away, but this customer has time to make sure it is precisely what is wanted.

SAD: Sandwich Aversion Disorder. (See chapter Secrets of Super Sandwich Making).

Sammie: Fond Australian colloquial for sandwich usually pluralised to "sammies" and very much associated with small bush towns. E.G. "Don't fergit yer sammies yer flamin' drongo" (or something like that). (See this chapter 'Sanger': and 'Sanga':)

Sammie Awards: Formerly the British National Annual Sandwich Industry Awards. An annual event organised by the BSA (See this chapter BSA:) to identify and reward innovators of recipes, equipment, service and marketing. It was during the writers tenure as Chairman of the BSA (2002) that this new name for the awards was proposed and adopted following his own suggestion.

The old name was "A bit of a mouthful" and the new name still raises a smile but in a positive way. As a footnote, renaming the Sandwich Awards was the only enduring contribution the writer can recall from his year in office. The Sammies now attracts in excess of 600 paying guests each year.

Samwich: Phonetic corruption of the word 'Sandwich'. Quite common UK wide even from those with the most correct and non regional accents.

Sandwedge: UK trade name for a sandwich packaging product patented by Spiral Packs Ltd. Cardboard alternative to plastic for factory made sandwiches allowing enhanced space to print for marketing purposes.

Sandwich Bags: Polythene bags 180mm X 230 mm sold from most cash and carry outlets in rolls of 500 or 250 specifically for wrapping or keeping sandwiches safe in transit. Also available in smaller retail packages. A useful and safe sandwich container but requiring a rigid box for travel to guard against squashing.

Sandwich Guide: This handy guide describes the sandwich formations used for running Moonstone Dies through the various die-cutting machines, to help achieve the perfect cut from your dies. Please note the smaller die-cutting machines may not accommodate the Moonstone Frame dies. Make sure to check the sizing of the die and your machine's dimensions before purchasing. * Author's note. This doesn't sound like anything to do with food at all. It is the result of Googling "sandwich guide". (See also Cutlebug Guide:)

Sandwich: A cold assembled hand-held bread snack using two or more slices of buttered bread with a layer of meat or cheese etc. in between. Named after John Montagu Fourth Earl of Sandwich (1718-1792), who ate food in this way rather than leave the gambling table to eat meals. (See 'Foreword' and chapter 'A Brief History of Sandwiches':)

Sandwich and Snack News: Former name of what is today "Sandwich and Food to Go News". Published by Trade Publications Ltd, the magazine (which some say "can't be gagged") has been the mouthpiece of the sandwich industry since 1990. Running to eighty odd pages six times per year with a circulation of around 6,000, sandwich aficionados are feasted on trade news, recipes, advertisements, business comment, profiles and a directory of accredited members of the British Sandwich Association. (See this chapter BSA:)

Sand in the Sandwiches: Delightful compendium of anecdotes, quotations and poetry performed live on stage by Edward Fox in celebration of the life and work of Sir John Betjeman.

Sandwich Bar: Shop or serving counter dedicated to the making, selling or serving of sandwiches.

Sandwich Bar of the Year: Award given annually by the BSA to what is in their view, the best sandwich bar in the UK.

Sandwich Bay: A picturesque stretch of coastline in Kent.

Sandwich Board: One of two connected boards usually bearing advertisements hung over the shoulders of one employed to parade.

Sandwich Box: Rigid container to protect sandwiches in transit.

Sandwich Cake: A cake that is made up of two or more layers of sponge with layers of jam or cream in between.

Sandwich Club, The: Marketing device aimed directly at consumers, promoted by the BSA and accessed via their website: www.sandwich.org.uk

Sandwich Compound: In chemistry, any of a class of organo-metallic compounds whose molecules have a metal atom or ion bound between two plane parallel organic rings.

Sandwich Course: Academic program consisting of periods of study alternating with periods of industrial or paid work.

Sandwich Day: USA. November 3rd - being the birthday of John Montagu the Fourth Earl of Sandwich in 1718.

Sandwich Digital Dispatch: Online news update from Sandwich and Food To Go News to BSA membership and subscribers. (See this chapter BSA :)

Sandwich, Earl of: Currently the Eleventh Earl is John Edward Hollister Montagu whose family seat, Mapperton, is near Beaminster in Dorset. His ancestor, the Fourth Earl, is said to have called for cuts of meat between slices of toasted bread to sustain him during a long session at the gaming table in 1762, thus giving his name to what is now called a sandwich.
(See Foreword and chapter *'A Brief History of Sandwiches':*)

Sandwiched: Being squeezed between two other events or objects in time or space, e.g. "My hair appointment is sandwiched between a driving lesson and violin practice".

Sandwich Islands: Name given to the Hawaiian Islands by Captain James Cook when he first sighted them from the deck of 'Resolution' on Sunday January 18th 1778. Cook was on his third and final voyage and making his way from Tahiti to Alaska for the start of the northern hemisphere spring when he made the discovery. He named the islands after Lord Montagu, the Fourth Earl of Sandwich who was a sponsor of the voyage. With so many new discoveries to name, Cook used the same names more than once, hence the South Sandwich Islands in the South Atlantic - see 'South Sandwich Islands'.

At first the local Hawaiians treated Cook like a god and called him Lono but he outstayed his welcome and was killed by the natives at Kealalekua Bay on Sunday February 14th 1779. Missionaries and 500 whalers arrived in 1820 and the USA formally annexed the islands in 1898 declaring them the 50th state on August 21st 1959 and renaming them Hawaii.

Sandwich Man: Person employed to wear and parade an advertising device, being two connected boards hung over the shoulders. (See this chapter 'Sandwich Board':)

Sandwich Pal: Range of sauces from US company Woeber including Horseradish Ketchup, Cranberry and Horseradish Ketchup and Mustard and Jalapeno Ketchup. Powerful flavours good for overwhelming bland ingredients. Better suited to hot dogs.

Sandwich Plates, set of: Usually four but occasionally six individual square china plates with one rectangular serving plate. Popular from late Victorian times and often highly decorated.

Sandwich Point: Southerly part of the volcanic South Sandwich Mountains of South Georgia in the South Atlantic.

Sandwich Round: Vending pattern adopted by one selling sandwiches, usually on foot, as in 'milk round'. Popular in areas poorly served by retailers, where the vendor carries sandwiches in baskets to the workplace. Such rounds can change hands for a consideration. Larger rounds and those covering industrial estates are usually motorised.

Sandwich Solutions Ltd: UK company solving sandwich problems.

Sandwich Spread: Particles of vegetable matter mixed into a binding agent resembling salad cream in taste and texture. This extraordinary material was the first manufactured recipe specifically for sandwiches, one of Heinz's original 57 varieties sold in glass jars and billed as "tangy and crunchy". It was withdrawn from sale in 1997 but then quickly re-introduced following an outcry from fans.

It remains today as 'Original Sandwich Spread' alongside 'Improved Recipe.' At least three further products have since appeared from the same company replacing the word 'spread' with 'Filler'. For those wishing to make it at home (not advised), the ingredients are as follows: Cabbage, sugar, spirit vinegar, vegetable oil, carrots, gherkins, (contains firming agent calcium chloride), modified corn flour, onions, egg yolks, red peppers, salt, mustard, mustard seeds, stabilisers (guagum and xanthan gum), spice extracts, spices, garlic extract, colour riboflavin, herb extract; quite a mouthful!

Sandwich Stage, the: Handle given to those in mid-life, between early love and fading middle age. Caring for one's children while looking after one's parents too. Divorced Dad Bill Douglas shares his emotions. "As a divorced entrepreneur, I'm working to create my own wealth and jobs for others. I know I'll find love again, there's absolutely no doubt in my mind. Right now I'm focused on being the best father I can be. And, because I'm in the sandwich stage, I'm doing my best to care for my aging parents, too."

Sandwich Tern: Sterno Sandvicensis. European tern with a yellow tipped bill, whitish plumage and white forked tail which nests in colonies on beaches.

Sanger: Fond contraction for a sandwich Down Under, being shortened from sangwich. (see below). "Beaut sangers Ma" from Australian Broadcasting Corporation's episodic soap opera 'Snake Gully'.

Sanga: Alternative spelling of "Sanger". (See this chapter 'Sanger':)

Sangwich: Irritating mispronunciation of sandwich. Common parlance in Scotland and to a lesser degree in Australia and NZ.

Sarnie: Countrywide UK slang term for a sandwich.

Sea Shanty Café: Unashamed plug for the writer's latest café/restaurant venture set in the dunes behind the main beach of Trearddur Bay, Anglesey. A monument to recycling, the seating area is cosy but spacious and dog friendly with several completely unique features. While serving excellent sandwiches, the fully licenced Sea Shanty is more than just a café, it serves superb food for breakfast, lunch and dinner. Email info@seashantycafe.co.uk.
Web www.seashantycafe.co.uk.
Telephone 01407 728 200.

Shark Sandwich: Vinyl album by Spinal Tap (Polymer Records 1980). 'Come back' record with mixed reviews including the two word comment "shit sandwich". This followed a promotion which included sending reviewers a real shark sandwich. History does not relate the full recipe nor any confirmation that each was accompanied by a card with the words " Bite on that Fritz".

Shawarma: Arabic:شاورما also spelled shawurma or shawerma, is a Levantine meat preparation, where lamb, chicken, turkey, beef, veal, or mixed meats are placed on a spit (commonly a vertical spit in restaurants), and may be grilled for as long as a day. Shavings are cut off the block of meat for serving, and the remainder of the block of meat is kept heated on the rotating spit. Shawarma can be served on a plate (generally with accompaniments), or as a sandwich or wrap. Shawarma is usually eaten with tabbouleh, fattoush, taboon bread, tomato, and cucumber. Toppings include tahini, hummus, pickled turnips, and amba. Shawarma is one of the world's most popular street foods, especially in the countries of the Levant and the Arabian Peninsula.

Related dishes in the region include Turkish döner kebab and Greek *gyros*.

Smorrebrod: Scandinavian sandwich.

Shelf-stable Pocket Sandwich: The US Army has developed shelf-stable pocket sandwiches as combat feeding rations (the First Strike Ration) for its troops on-the-go. These sandwiches are engineered to prevent microbial growth through the use of specialized water treatment, acidic content (naturally, through ingredient selection; or by the addition of food-grade acids), special multi-layer foil packaging, and oxygen-absorbing packets. Mmmmmm yummy.

Snack: Light intake of food synonymous with packeted savoury products but also associated with sandwiches.

Snacking: The habit of eating light snacks at times other than traditional meal times.

Snapping (also Snappin' and Snap): Noun referring to packed lunch. Derives either from the opening and closing of the lid of the container or the opening and closing of the jaws of the consumer. "Is it snapping time yet?".

Snodding: Act of breaking open a loaf and sniffing it to tell the quality of the dough and bake.

South Sandwich Islands: A group of inhospitable islands (almost only populated by penguins and research scientists) located in Antartica. On visiting their shores in 1775, Captain James Cook was moved to describe them as "The most awful place in the world". Should not be confused with the Sandwich Islands now called Hawaii. (See this chapter 'Sandwich Islands':)

St. James Sandwich: As described by Mrs Beeton in her 19th century publication 'Household Management', what today we would call vol-au -vent having no bread but an ingredient preparation enclosed in a puff pastry parcel.

Stottie: Stottie cake. Large round flat loaf made with extra lard peculiar to the North East of England, particularly Newcastle Upon Tyne. Made into one huge sandwich it can be cut into four or six wedge shaped portions which are offered for sale individually. Most popular ingredient is Cheese Savoury.

Sub: USA only. Shortened from 'Submarine', which describes the shape of a long bread roll used to contain ingredients.

Sunday Sandwich: In cricket; two games played over a weekend.

TBE: Turkey, Bacon, Emmenthal (or Swiss).

The Big Cheese: Medieval term of respect referring to someone wealthy enough, or having enough servants to justify buying whole wheels or truckles of cheese at a time.

The Big Sandwich: Light - hearted term by which any current chairman of the BSA is known. (See this chapter 'BSA':)

The meat in the Sandwich: Morose reflection from one who finds him or herself between two irreconcilable opposing forces.

The Sandwich Man: 1966. British light comedy starring Michael Medwin.

Tartine: France. Another name for a sandwich made with a single slice of bread. Sometimes called just an open sandwich, also known as an open-face/open-faced breadplatter or tartine. It consists of a single slice of bread with one or more food items on top. (See also this chapter 'Open Sandwich':)

Total Sandwich Show: Two day trade guzzle ...

Bap: Unsophisticated round white bread roll...

*"Of course, there isn't anything
very interesting inside."*

'The Sandwich': Handshake involving both hands with a caressing action by the thumb of the right hand. Described by former Conservative MP Theresa Gorman as "the most intimate", it sits with other notorious handshakes such as 'The Cup', 'The Pat', 'The Vice', 'The Doorbell', and of course "The Wet Fish'. "Was he/she pleased to see you?" "Yes, he/she gave me 'the sandwich'."

Toastie: Shortened from 'Toasted Sandwich'. Generally low form of the latter rarely straying beyond cheese and tomato or ham and cheese. Popular with pub landlords for their simplicity of preparation and ability to mollify drunks.

Torta: Mexican sandwich made in a crusty or soft roll with fried or marinated pork, jalapenos, avocado and mayonnaise. Other ingredients include marinated steak and cheese.

Total Sandwich Show, The: Two day trade guzzle for the sandwich industry held at Olympia giving producers, packagers, manufacturers, equipment suppliers and food companies the opportunity to sell products and services. Operated by Dew Events Ltd in association with the BSA. (See this chapter 'BSA':)

Town of Sandwich, UK: Situated in Kent, it is famous amongst other things as the town where Viagra was invented!

Town of Sandwich, USA (i): Located in Barnstable County in the Northwest corner of Cape Cod, Massachusetts. Population 22,000, it describes itself as a "quaint old seaside town and an attractive place to visit".

Town of Sandwich, USA (ii): Found nestling in the State of New Hampshire and divided into five separate communities: 'Sandwich', 'Centre Sandwich', 'North Sandwich', 'East Sandwich' and finally, 'West Sandwich'.

Town of Sandwich, USA (iii): Small community found in Illinois. Nothing more known .

To Sandwich: Verb. The verb "To sandwich" was first used over 200 years ago and meant "to have a light lunch" a bit like saying "lets picnic". Today the word is associated more with the make up of the food than with the habits of the 4th Earl of Sandwich. "Squeeze between" being the modern meaning of "to sandwich".

Tram Lining: Sandwich manufacturing term. The streaky effect of butter on bread when the automatic buttering machine becomes blocked with bread crumbs so preventing an even spread.

Triple Decker Sandwich: Having three slices of bread and two layers of ingredients which, strictly speaking should be the same, unlike a Club Sandwich in which the two layers differ. In this case, the 'decks' refer to the number of slices of bread.

Trivia: Latin. Literally trivia or 'three roads'. From the Roman method of disseminating small pieces of news: or useful (or not so useful) facts by posting notices at road junctions. Here mentioned because this book contains so much.

Vada Pav: Indian vegetarian sandwich. The vada is a ball of hot spiced mashed potato flattened into the shape of a burger, then battered and deep fried. Placed in a burger type bun (called a pav) the 'patty' can now be treated with chutneys and sauces in varieties like only the Indians can make. Delicious.

VCB: Vertically Cut Bun. Roll or baguette with ingredients partially stuffed down into a vertical slot instead of lying between a 'top' and a 'bottom'. The technique creates a dazzling appearance of cornucopian plenty but rarely fulfils its promise, leaving the eater hungry and trying to wipe salad cream off the end of his or her nose. More or less confined to tourist attractions, airlines and other economy driven mass catering venues.

Vegemite Sandwich: Cultural linchpin for Australians, much as the peanut butter and jelly is for Americans. Vegemite is the trade name for an Australian made yeast extract spread similar to Marmite but containing no animal content.

Wedge: Tri-cornered plastic packet into which manufactured sandwiches are put for storage, display and sale. Hand closed with a flip top lid, it wasn't until Hans Blokmann invented the Easy Peel Sandwich Skillet or 'Cono seal' in 1985 that sandwich manufacturers were able to package sandwiches as fast as they could make them.

Wrap: Ingredients enclosed in a flour tortilla offering a different texture and yeast free substitute for bread. Product offered to the sandwich market and sold by sandwich shops as an ancillary line.

Buying a sandwich.
Top tips.

No.1: Never buy pub sandwiches on a Sunday. The bread will usually be yesterdays.

No.2: Always avoid VCBs or VCRs (See chapter A-Z:)

No. 3: Eating while driving is of course illegal. However, if one has brought or bought a sandwich to eat in a lay by, make sure it is not a Banjo Sandwich (See chapter A-Z. Banjo sandwich:)

No.4: Anybody making a sandwich with an ordinary piece of metal cutlery such as a knife or fork doesn't know what they are doing. Watch out for painful spreading, pathetic portions and a long wait.

No.5: If faced with a poor choice of ready-made sandwiches and what looks like tired slightly browning salad, and no alternative shop. Choose egg mayonnaise. It is very hard for a manufacturer to screw this up completely because of the nature of egg.

No. 6: When buying an egg sandwich, see if salt or pepper portions are available because there will most likely be little or no seasoning included in the manufacture and therefore little or no flavour in what you are buying.

No. 7: If you are trying to cut down on carbs, here is a useful way to stave off hunger and also actually enjoy a low end product (bought possibly from a garage). Holding a wedge vertically, cut face down, gently remove the crusts peeling them upwards and discard. This is quite easy to do and usually demonstrates that there wasn't actually any ingredient in the strips you have removed . Now you have all of the ingredients and none of the extra carb. The 'ingredient to bread' ratio has improved way beyond what the manufacturer ordained and there is less carb and less chewing.

No.8: When moving in unfamiliar territory, a foreign town, a funfair, weekly market situation, London, and you want to buy some food on the go, follow this top tip. Spare a moment to glance at litter bins. Their contents will tell you what the worst offer nearby is. It may also tell you by the number of neatly folded discarded empty containers what the most popular local offer is likely to be too.

No.9: Low end sandwich bars usually offer low end bulk bought in grated cheddar cheese. Unless you can direct sufficient mayonnaise in the correct manner, you will have a banjo (See chapter A-Z Banjo Sandwich:) situation on your hands. One is better buying a small amount of cheese from a shop, deli or supermarket and stuffing it into a bap/roll probably bought at the same shop. EG. A mini Camembert costing £1.20 stuffed into a single bap from a packet of 4 costing 60p will be a better eat and cheaper lunch.

sandwich statistics

Enough bread is produced from one acre of good wheat to feed the average family of four on sandwiches for ten years.

Bread really does tend to land butter side down when dropped on account of the butter side being heavier.

Scandinavian tradition holds that if a boy and girl eat sandwiches made from the same loaf, they are bound to fall in love.

People will buy a sandwich approximately seven times more often than they will buy a Chinese takeaway.

In the UK, approximately six chicken sandwiches are eaten each second.

In the USA National Sandwich Day is November 3rd. This compares poorly with the UK which sets aside an entire week every May. November 3rd was the Fourth Earl of Sandwich's birthday,

The earliest known use of the word Sandwich was in 1494. It appears to have meant some kind of chord.

More sandwiches are eaten in hot weather than in cold.

Nearly 12 billion sandwiches are eaten annually in the UK. Of these more than half are made at home and half of those also eaten at home.

The most popular choices of bought sandwiches in the UK are:- Cheese, ham and chicken in that order.

£7.6 billion. This is the current annual spend on shop bought sandwiches in the UK.

In times of stress, surveys show that the bacon 'butty' brings greater comfort than all others.

Bacon Sandwiches (according to researchers at Newcastle University), can cure a hangover. They claim it boosts the level of amines which speeds up the metabolism and clears the head.

In the UK, sandwiches outsell every other form of fast food, accounting for 42 percent of all convenience food sales.

Approximately 8.2 billion sandwiches are eaten every year in Britain. At an average of six inches each, corner to corner, if placed in a line touching each other they would stretch to the moon and back.

More people are employed by the UK sandwich industry than in the whole of British agriculture. Approximately 300,000 people.

The cost of a tank of petrol bought twenty years ago would buy five sandwiches from a filling station today.

The word 'sandwich', 'sandwiches', or 'sandwiched' appears precisely 661 times in this book. (See Chapter 'Record Sandwiches':)

Carry out: Meal made at home and taken out

Meaticus Carryouta

Sarni

Romans and Normans... Ploughman's and Hellmann's.

a brief history of sandwiches

Sandwiches BC

The concept of sandwiches is probably as old as bread itself, and bread is very, very old. The ancient Romans, Greeks and Egyptians almost certainly served slices of meat, tomatoes and cheese on bread, probably an unleavened form which didn't need slicing. In cultures without bread, there is always an equivalent cereal based food staple with which to enclose or accompany food. In India for example, it is the chapatti, dosa or naan, in Mexico the tortilla or enchilada. Pitta for the middle East and in the Horn of Africa they create a large thick sheet of starchy food called injera using millet and vinegar. The latter acts as plate, knife and fork, glove and food accompaniment all rolled into one.

Confining ourselves to Northern Europe, it is important to remember that until Josiah Wedgewood and others began mass producing tableware in the mid 18th century, only the very wealthy and aristocracy used cutlery and crockery at all. So what did everyone else do?

The short answer is they used bread. Tearing a flat loaf (called a trencher) horizontally produced two 'plates', his and hers perhaps? Crust down, into the exposed 'bread' side could be poured a ladle of stew from the pot. Just as in many parts of the world today, deft use of the fingers and more pieces of bread are used to transport the food from the 'plate' to the mouth. When the meat is gone, the bread contains all the juices and gravy, and this is then consumed to eliminate waste completely and finish the meal. It also took care of the washing up.

Different shaped loaves are still used for different foods in different parts of the world. Clam chowder is popular in the north-east USA served in a hollowed out loaf, and a similar idea to contain hot potato chips is popular in parts of Wales.

The Romans described an assortment of different cheeses (and other foods) they found in lands freshly conquered and it is difficult to imagine these being eaten without some kind of carrier to accompany and dilute this powerful food. However comical the image, we cannot avoid the strong possibility that when the appropriate moment arrived for a food halt, a marching legion sat down and unpacked sandwiches.

A Light Lunch to end the Dark Ages

The Normans brought their interest in food with them when in 1066 they took over Britain. It is no accident that much of our language that describes food in its finished prepared state is derived from French, while in its unprepared state, still 'on the hoof', derives from Anglo Saxon. For example, 'Mutton' from the French 'mouton' when cooked sounds nothing like sheep, and 'beef' from the French 'boef' when cooked sounds nothing like cow.

The Norman interest in food and influence upon our culture was huge. Then as now they baked good bread as befitted their interest in 'cuisine'. Almost certainly they would have had some form of filled baguette to take on their hunting trips about which they were passionate.

In the middle ages, wooden plates also called trenchers were increasingly used to serve food, with wooden bowls for soup and broth. However, bread was never far away just as it still accompanies a meal no matter which restaurant you eat in no matter the time of day. It is easy to see how, what we know as a sandwich developed.

The need for food to be portable, and not requiring utensils to eat it with, is still seen in foods like the sausage roll, oggey or Cornish pasty where the roped twist of pastry on top serves as a handle. Food safety probably came into it a bit too, particularly with the Cornish pasty, the 'handle' was not eaten thus preventing contamination from less than clean farm workers' or tin miners' hands.

A 'ploughman's lunch' had and has all the elements of today's classic sandwich - cheese, lettuce, tomato, pickle and bread and the migration to a cheese and onion salad sandwich with pickle is not difficult to imagine .

Presumably ploughmen were not exposed to the same sort of bacterial dangers as those eating a Cornish pasty.

What's in a name?

In all its forms, the sandwich has become increasingly a deeply entrenched part of the British way of life. From delicate cucumber sandwiches served for tea on the lawn after tennis, to thick doorsteps crammed into the lunch boxes of workers in the 1940s and 50s, sandwiches cut across class barriers like a knife through butter.

The cachet of giving a title to something basic, particularly food, was an accident of history waiting to happen and in the 18th century, the sandwich became fashionable not only in England but in Europe too. But who was this Sandwich?

The Fourth Earl of Sandwich

John Montagu, the Fourth Earl of Sandwich was born in 1718 and became First Lord of the Admiralty in 1748. It is said of him that he rebuilt the British Navy, but that America was lost 'on his watch'.
He was educated at Eton, and later entered Cambridge, but left without a degree to undertake a 'Grand Tour of Europe' which was considered essential education for well born young men at the time. Nowadays it's called a gap year. The tour was a success and apart from the usual broadening of the mind, the Earl returned with a substantial collection of coins and archaeological remains. In 1739 he was elected to the Royal Society and entered the House of Lords. From 1744 he occupied numerous military posts, and in 1776 as first Lord of the Admiralty, outfitted and dispatched Captain Cook on his third round the world voyage of discovery.

The Earl and Martha Ray

In 1778 the Earl's mistress since 1762, a popular singer called Martha Ray, was murdered by 'an unbalanced clergyman' who wanted to marry her. Approaching her one night after her performance at the opera, the man shot her in the head for which he was later hanged. Martha was a well-known singer and it is believed that she may have been the inspiration for the female lead in the musical 'My Fair Lady'. The Earl's own wife suffered from progressive mental problems and in 1767 she was made a ward of court after being insane for over two years.

Deeply affected by the condition of his wife and by Martha's death, the Earl dutifully acknowledged his mistress' children, two of whom rose to great prominence. Basil became a lawyer, responsible for much of the foundations of English bankruptcy law, and Rodger became an Admiral.

The Earl 'invents' the sandwich

Strictly speaking, it is wrong to attribute the invention of sandwiches to Sandwich. Folding or enclosing ingredients between slices of bread, as we have already seen had probably been around for centuries.

Clearly the convenience of eating sandwiches suited the Earls '24 /7' lifestyle and he ate them often.

It is easy to imagine the Earl's friends teasing him about a way of eating that was, at the time, unconventional for gentlemen of his class, and easy to see why they used his name to describe the habit.

No doubt those who lovingly prepared these meals, perhaps Martha Ray who was herself a good cook, sought ways of enhancing the experience.

These people played a role in developing sandwiches just as domestic and commercial sandwich makers do today.

This said, it is appropriate to quote N.A.M. Roger's definitive biography 'The Insatiable Earl: A Life of John Montagu' on the subject. He writes: *"It remains to consider the circumstances of the invention of the sandwich, which modern works supposed to have been designed to sustain its creator through long nights at the gaming table. The origins of this story seem to be a passage in Grosley's Tour to London:*

"A minister of the state passed four and twenty hours at a public gaming table, so absorbed in play that, during the whole time, he had no subsistence but a bit of beef, between two slices of toasted bread, which he eats without ever quitting the game. This new dish grew highly in vogue, during my residence in London: it was called by the name of the minister who invented it."

Grosley's book is a piece of travel literature ... there is no supporting evidence for this gossip, especially as it refers to 1765 when Sandwich was a Cabinet minister and very busy. There is no doubt, however that he was the real author of the sandwich, in its original form using salt beef, of which he was very fond.

The alternative explanation is that he invented it to sustain himself at his desk, which seems since we have ample evidence of the long hours he worked ... in an age when dinner was the only substantial meal of the day, and the fashionable hour to dine was four o'clock."

It should be remembered however, that the lower classes probably ate food in this form all the time. It was Sandwiches standing and elevated position that made the habit acceptable to the upper classes.

The Earl and the Hell Fire Club

Sandwich was also a principal member of the Hell Fire Club, also known as the Monks of Medmenham, a risque secret society with esoteric interests that only the cleverest of his associates were invited to join. Created by Sir Francis Dashwood, members originally met in the caves beneath the ancient Abbey of Medmenham, which they could reach by boat from the river under cover of darkness. Workmen were sent in to rebuild the abbey and landscape the grounds into a 'garden of lust'.

Marble pillars were erected on which were inscribed pornographic inscriptions in bastard or 'macaroni ' Latin. Small Grecian style temples were put up and the groves were filled with statuary in indecent poses. The abbey's library supposedly contained one of the most complete collections of pornography in England.

For the monks there were nuns, most of whom were prostitutes, or local girls in search of excitement, and even society ladies. Many nuns were the wives, mothers, or sisters of members, many of whom were among the most prominent men in the kingdom. The influence of the group on world affairs prompted Benjamin Franklin to become a monk sometime after his arrival in England in 1764.

The Earl and Joseph Banks

In the Endeavour journals of Joseph Banks (edited by John Beaglehole (See chapter 'Further Reading':) there are numerous references to Sandwich. This one is interesting:

"Mrs Banks (Joseph's mother} moved to London, or rather Chelsea, to a pleasant house in Paradise Walk near the Apothecaries' Garden that Sir Hans Sloane had founded not so many years before. It was an excellent situation for botanical vacations. It had also the advantage of the neighbourhood of one whose Huntingdonshire country seat was not far from Lincolnshire, John Motagu, fourth Earl of Sandwich, a man who, though twenty five years older than Banks, became his fast friend. Sandwich had for many years already been deep in politics, his acquaintance with the world was wide and his way of thinking - to blunt the point of many accusations against him -liberal; to a talent for genial foolery he united a great intelligence, in spite of his rather peculiar deep-jawed face, and extreme personal charm - a charm, indeed, even more winning and certainly more stable than that of Banks. He was to be useful to Banks, and he was, it seems, to form a pretty accurate estimate of some at least of the capacities of his young friend . Sandwich was capable of sharing a botanical expedition and both were passionate fishermen.

*Possibly it is to their association of this
period, possibly to some years later, that we may refer
to a story that seems to have given the mature Banks a
great deal of pleasure: "So zealous were both these
friends in the prosecution of the sport (Jocular foolery
and fishing}, that Sir Joseph used to tell of a project
that they had formed for suddenly draining the
Serpentine by letting off the water; and he was wont to
lament their scheme being discovered the night before
it was to have been executed: their hope was to have
thrown much light on the state and habits of the fish".
Their expectation for profitable research by this
radical method is so tenuous that it is much more likely
their hope was to have thrown confusion on London."*

By all accounts the Fourth Earl of Sandwich was a
colourful man who lived life to the full. Taller than
average, he cut a dash walking down the street with a
girl on each arm, the Earl 'sandwiched' between the
two. His carousing and gambling were legendary and
it is no wonder the public quickly took the
opportunity to attach his name to something as
enjoyable as a sandwich.
He died in 1792 at the age of 74.

Where are they now?

The current eleventh Earl of Sandwich is John Edward Hollister Montagu who lives at the family seat near Beaminster in Dorset with his family. His second son the Honourable Orlando Montagu, after a break of just 239 years has brought the Sandwich family back into sandwiches with a commercial venture called, surprisingly, 'Earl of Sandwich'.

20th Century Sandwich

It is difficult to know when the first sandwich bars appeared but it is highly likely it was on the continent. While British people bought fish and chips, tea and toast and the occasional slice of cake, sandwiches were something made at home. British Railways were forced to offer some kind of catering for passengers, and succeeded in giving sandwiches a reputation so bad it took 40 years to shake off. This left the field clear for pizzas, burgers, Chinese, Indian, Middle Eastern and other ethnic foods and with all the excitement, nobody had time to think about that dried up old sandwich.

Slowly in the fifties, one or two little sandwich shops appeared in the city of London catering for office workers.

Operated mainly by Italian migrants who one suspects brought the idea with them, or had heard about it from relatives in America where things had developed earlier, their popularity gathered pace and by the end of the sixties they were common in most parts of the capital. However, in regional towns, sandwiches were still pre made (by hand), probably wrapped in cling film, and served from bakeries and cafes and even petrol stations. But they lacked quality.

In Britain' s smaller towns, bakeries were the obvious starting point for those looking for something to eat without having to sit down and wait to be served. By the end of the sixties most bread shops had some kind of sandwich offer, usually made on the premises and displayed often without refrigeration. Choice did not stray much beyond ham, cheese or egg.

About this time garage forecourts too attempted to meet the demand of people (motorists) who needed to eat but couldn't afford the time or money to sit down in a cafe or restaurant. Held in ambient temperature and made with poor quality ingredients, these offers were a fresh blow to the public's image of a bought sandwich.

During the 1970s, standards slowly improved especially in London where, with the growing availability of fresh and interesting produce from the continent, and healthy competition, sandwich bars thrived.

There was a growing demand for food that could be bought and brought back to the office to be eaten. Meanwhile at home, consumers discovered Hellmann's Real Mayonnaise which improved sandwiches enormously. Mayonnaise quickly replaced Salad Cream to become the single most useful sandwich ingredient after bread.

In 1981, Marks and Spencer established themselves as the first credible offer of packaged sandwiches. All the other supermarket chains would follow over the next few years but M&S remains the name that is most remembered for its revolutionary offer. Prawn and mayonnaise.

Birley

Then in 1982 came a dramatic development. A young man called Robin Birley opened a sandwich shop in Fenchurch Street, London that radically brought sandwiches into the realms of 'posh nosh'. He persevered with suppliers to introduce crispy bacon for the first time, made his own mayonnaise on the premises, sought out high quality breads and used Limoges china instead of the customary plastic.

With the city booming and every sandwich made with generous amounts of quality ingredients, it wasn't long before there were five Birley shops with queues down the street. Prices were high but so was value, and nobody cared because the sandwiches were so delicious and the city was booming too.

Inspired by spectacular offers in Australia, where migrant influences mixed with a bountiful climate and economy had produced some of the best fast food in the world, and having observed Birley's success in London, the author opened Philpotts first shop in 1985 in the City of Chester. It was the first shop exclusively selling sandwiches to open outside London. It is still there and, at the time of writing, so is one of the original staff, Pam Owens who became something of a legend herself.

Among its 36 standard offers was Coronation chicken, actually it was referred to as Chicken Coronation. The recipe was taken from one devised to mark the coronation of Queen Elizabeth 11. The original involved large chunks of chicken smeared in a delicious faintly curried dressing. Philpotts shredded the chicken into strips such that it combined with the strips of onion in the coronation mixture and acquired a suitably 'squashy' texture perfectly adapted to be a sandwich ingredient. Topped with a locally made Indian chutney, this sandwich quickly became famous locally. Today "Coronation Chicken" is available as a sandwich worldwide.

In 1999 Philpotts began building Juice and Smoothie bars into its shops. It was ahead of its time in so doing, but smoothies in particular are now a thoroughly accepted product and available everywhere.

In 1985 when Philpotts first opened its door (June 4th) The average price of its sandwiches was £1.05 while most sandwiches on offer from nearby bakeries were sold for less than 45p. With a culture of constant improvement, the addition of carvery bars, coffee and juice bars plus a 'ready to go' offer and gourmet soups, Philpotts enjoyed an unrivalled reputation with staff and customers and by 2002 was in every major city centre in England EXCEPT London. Publicity from a series of awards brought hundreds of visitors scouting for ideas (including Marks and Spencer) and today the influence of this small chain is visible on menus, equipment, interior design and 'system of service' in sandwich bars all over Britain and occasionally abroad.

In 1983, two London estate agents, Sinclair Beecham and Julian Metcalf recognised that a degree of complacency with regard to innovative sandwich ingredients had opened a new niche in London. Coupled with a 'ready made' system of service which was considerably more efficient than the 'made to order' procedure, their first Pret a Manger shop was an instant success. Over the next ten years they opened more than a hundred shops and were honoured by the Queen for "services to catering". There are now aproximately 500 'Prets' in nine countries.

1987 brought a stock market crash which imposed unemployment on many of Birley's customers while opening a new market for thrifty eaters. Benjy's inexpensive offer of ready-made sandwiches and rolls became popular with all classes and a chain of 38 shops grew quickly. Sadly, the company folded when the economy recovered and nobody wanted a cheap sandwich.

Regulations

With the arrival of food handling regulations, and determination on the part of the industry, garage forecourts raised their standards too, introducing properly chilled environments from which to vend factory made, date and ingredient labelled safe sandwiches. By the 1990s, the stage was set for a booming industry.

Today, production technology, shortened lunchbreaks, improved recipes and marketing have spawned a giant arm of the service and hospitality industry. Sandwich bars jostle with building societies and clothes shops for space on the high street and sandwiches form a vital part of the offer of every big-name retailer. Despite all this, of the estimated 8.2 billion sandwiches eaten in Britain every year, 5.4 billion of them are made at home. While 'new world' foods rise and fall in popularity, sandwiches, with their original staple ingredients endure and at the time of writing the sandwich market continues to grow at a steady 2% per annum.

Back to Europe

In 2002 mainland Europe was tooling up to join the boom. As people crammed ever more into their crowded lives, the demand for a hand held healthy snack continued to grow. Britain began exporting expertise and marketing experience to the continent on a grand scale as Europeans scrambled to embrace the essentially British sandwich.

It was at this time that Sandwich and Snack news (BSA organ of the sandwich industry) renamed itself International Sandwich and Snack News. Today it is called International Sandwich and Food to Go News.

Today

Just as coffee shops have become so popular, sandwich bars have continued to abound. Franchises such as O'Briens from Ireland, Subway from the USA, join in with supermarkets, petrol stations and chemists to sell an ever-widening range of sandwich offers.

Other 'snacks' have grown alongside sandwiches, such as yoghurts with fruit or granola, wraps, flatbreads, juices and smoothies. The above offers are everything a working person needs to be able to fit lunch into 28 minutes, which is how long the average lunch 'hour' now is. These foods not only allow working people to work through lunch, but after work and before work ie breakfast and tea.

The new challenge is to find a way to fulfil the remaining 'day part' which sandwiches have not yet managed to break into…. dinner.

Internationally, some form of grain carriage/vehicle to embrace a protein ingredient has been traditional for an unrecorded length of time. It may be a flour tortilla, chapati, pastry case (pasty or sausage roll), taco, pancake or one of a thousand different forms of bread.

The writer has observed that while the 'carrier' remains constant, the universal expansion of generic ingredients in a shrinking world is manifest.

Hotdog:...'Poor quality food but tempting in the extreme...'

"Don't wrap it up I'll take one bite and throw it away here".

famous sandwiches

Pastrami on Rye

Pastrami is beef cured in brine and vinegar. As a sandwich, it became popular amongst the Jewish community of New York served on Rye bread with mustard and dill pickle. In 1888, Katz deli on the Lower East Side of Manhattan, New York, was opened by a Russian migrant family and quickly became a refuge of taste for thousands of migrants looking for reminders of the Old World.

Today Katz still makes the best pastrami sandwich the writer has found. Still hanging from the ceiling is the sign made famous in several films and documentaries since the war: "Send a salami to your boy in the army".

Reuben

Served cold or grilled, this American favourite of corned beef, melted Swiss cheese, mustard, Russian (or Thousand Island) dressing, sauerkraut on rye bread is typically over filled and of uncertain origin. Aficionados insist you never use cheddar cheese on a Reuben. Supposedly named after Arthur Reuben whose once famous sandwich deli in New York no longer exists.

Legend has it that the sandwich was created in 1914 for the actress Annette Seelos who was in the lead role of a Charlie Chaplin film being shot at the time. There is an alternative story, which has the Reuben being invented by one Reuben Kay during a game of poker in 1955. Kay, an Omaha wholesale grocer had an employee who won a national sandwich competition using this recipe and thus brought it fame. The poker game story sounds to the writer like a US bid to hijack the popular 'Earl of Sandwich at the gaming table' legend of 200 years earlier.

Cheese and Onion

Rural Britain's (and the writer's) favourite sandwich with or without pickle, chutney or mayonnaise. These two ingredients are the ultimate complimentary combination of fat and acid. An industry challenge (with a purse of £1,000) to produce a method of growing square onions to facilitate this sandwich was offered by the writer during his term as Chairman of the BSA. There were no takers.

Coronation Chicken

This 1953 recipe, created for the coronation of Oueen Elizabeth 11, first appeared on a sandwich bar menu in June, 1985.

Served with Indian apple chutney and salad, it quickly became famous among sandwich aficionados in and around the locality of Chester in Cheshire where it first appeared. Spotted by a Marks and Spencer scout two years later, Coronation Chicken is now universally known, made and enjoyed across the UK and indeed the world, as a sandwich ingredient.

The sandwich bar in Chester that pioneered what was then a highly unusual sandwich was called Philpotts.

Because customers continually asked staff what it was, they (staff) were taught to repeat the recipe word perfectly in reply. The words were "The raw chicken is boiled in water infused with bouquet garni and lemon, then taken off the bone and torn into strips. Onions are sliced and cooked in butter until clear then apricot jam and vindaloo paste are added. Now the mixture is combined with the chicken and folded together with mayonnaise."

"I ain't goin' to work on Maggie's barm no more"

sandwiches on stage

'Mama' Cass Elliot, the American star of rock group the 'Mamas and the Papas' was believed by many to have died choking on a ham sandwich. The truth is that she died from a heart attack in her hotel room in London on July 29th, 1974 and a post-mortem found there to be no traces of food in her trachea whatsoever.

The ham sandwich legend started apparently when the first doctor to reach the scene of the overweight singer's demise apparently told journalists that a sandwich was found on her nightstand. An indeterminate sandwich in the seventies was most likely to be described as "ham".
Source: *Fortean Times*

"Marmite sandwiches on the sand, and sand on the Marmite sandwiches".
Alan Bennett and Jonathan Miller: 'Beyond the Fringe'

"...I said do you speak-a-my-language... She just smiled and gave me a Vegemite sanguage.. ."
(See chapter A-Z of Sandwiches 'Sanguage':) From the number one hit 'Land Down Under' by Australian rock band **Men at Work**.

"In Spain, attempting to obtain a chicken-salad sandwich, you wind up with a dish whose name, when you look it up in your Spanish-English dictionary, turns out to mean 'Eel with the big abscess'."
Dave Barry

"One of the most popular Soviet meals is the Bread Sandwich, That is, two slices of bread with another slice of bread inbetween. They have the same thing in America - it's called a 'Big Mac'."
Yakov Smirnoff

During British Sandwich Week 2002, the Sunday Mirror reported the following sandwich preferences from well known personalities.

The Hamiltons: Christine and Neil like "Nutty seedy brown bread with avocado and stilton or strong Cheddar with tangy pickle"

Joan Collins: "Tuna on white bread"

Lesley Walters: "Cream cheese, smoked bacon, blue- berries and maple syrup on a bagel"

Rosemary Conley: "Lean beef, horseradish and Parmesan shavings and no butter"

Richard Wilson: "Chicken and avocado on Granary bread"

Rick Wakeman: "Thick cut lean ham with a large dollop of English mustard on Granary bread"

Dale Winton: "BLT"

As part of his estimated 23,000 calories per day intake of food, **Elvis Presley's** favourite sandwich was reported to be deep fried peanut butter and banana. Made in three sizes [small, large and King), the recipe is detailed in 'Are You Hungry Tonight?' a cook book on sale at Gracelands. The bread is lightly toasted then, with the ingredients firmly sandwiched, fried in butter on both sides until brown. Nigella Lawson mentions it in one of her books and, not being a fan of either peanut butter or bananas herself, speaks rapturously of the flavour in spite of the "Kamikaze calories".

Le Sandwich Anglaise...

"...taking snacking to new heights..."
'Sandwich and Snack News'

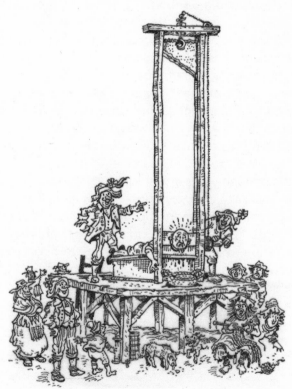

"Its only egg mayo..it won't kill you.."

sandwiches
at war

An 'Indestructible Sandwich' has been developed by
the US Army which stays fresh for three years.
Available in Pepperoni or Barbecue Chicken, the
breakthrough was announced in April, 2002 following
a tough survival programme which included air drops,
extreme heat and heavy impact. Despite these rigours,
these chunky sandwiches developed by food
scientists at the Army Soldier System Centre in
Nantucket, Massachusetts, are designed to remain
tasty and fresh sealed in a laminated pouch after
months or even years in a soldier's knapsack.
Longevity is achieved by using chemicals called
humectants which, when applied to the bread and
other ingredients, have the double effect of preventing
dehydration while hampering the growth of bacteria.
The product was scheduled to go into action in 2004.
There are no more details but Wellington always said
that an army marches on its stomach.

The start of World War 1, world war 2, the atom
bomb, all the result of one man feeling hungry and
going to buy a sandwich? Well the story goes like this:-

It is the summer of 1914, and Bosnia has just become part of the Austro-Hungarian empire. A handful of young Bosnian-born Serbs decide to strike a blow for the integration of their people into a Greater Serbia by assassinating the heir to the Austrian throne. Their opportunity comes when it is announced that Franz Ferdinand will be making a state visit to the provincial capital, Sarajevo.

Armed with bombs and pistols supplied by Serbian military intelligence, seven conspirators position themselves at intervals along the archduke's route. The first to strike is Nedeljko Cabrinovic, who lobs a hand grenade toward Franz Ferdinand's open touring car. But the grenade is an old one, with a 10-second fuse. It bounces off the limo and into the road, where it explodes under the next vehicle in the motorcade.

Although several officers in that car are hurt, Franz Ferdinand remains uninjured. To avoid capture, Cabrinovic drains a vial of cyanide and throws himself into a nearby river—but his suicide bid fails. The cyanide is past its sell-by date, and the river is just four inches deep.

The bombing throws the rest of the day's plans into disarray. The motorcade is abandoned. Franz Ferdinand is hurried off to the town hall, where he is due to meet with state officials.

Disconsolate, the remaining assassins disperse, their chance apparently gone. One of them, Gavrilo Princip, heads for Moritz Schiller's delicatessen, on Franz Joseph Street. It's one of Sarajevo's smartest shopping destinations, just a few yards from the bustling through road known as Appel Quay.

As Princip queues to buy a sandwich, Franz Ferdinand is leaving the town hall. When the heir gets back into his limousine, though, he decides on a change of plan—he'll call at the hospital to visit the men injured in the grenade blast.

There's just one problem: the archduke's chauffeur, a stranger to Sarajevo, gets lost. He swings off Appel Quay and into crowded Franz Joseph Street, then drifts to a stop right in front of Schiller's.

Princip looks up from his lunch to find his target sitting just a few feet away. He pulls his gun. Two shots ring out, and the first kills Franz Ferdinand's wife, Sophie. The second hits the heir in the neck, severing his jugular vein.

The archduke slumps back, mortally wounded. His security men hustle Princip away. Inside Schiller's deli, the most important sandwich in the history of the world lies half-eaten on a table.

sandwiches in science

N=C+ { fb (cm). fb (tc) } + fb (ts) + fc. ta.
This is the formula for the perfect bacon sandwich say scientists at Leeds University.

The secret to the perfect bacon butty, according to this research, is not the sauce or loving care put into assembly, it is the implementation of the above formula for cooking time and temperature which produces the crunchiest of results. And that crispiness, according to research is the most crucial characteristic of a perfect bacon sandwich. The author is in full agreement but admits that the RIGHT bacon cooked but STILL SOFT can SOMETIMES produce a good experience if the bread and other elements are correct. But crispy is king.

700 variations of the traditional bacon butty were tried by experts at Leeds University. They used different kinds of bacon, cooking techniques, types of oil, and a range of cooking times at different temperatures.

A shortlist was tested for texture by computers and then given to 50 volunteers to rate.

The results according to research team leader Dr Graham Clayton showed that a crispy bacon ingredient was the key. "We often think that it's the taste and smell of bacon that consumers find most attractive but our research proves that texture and the sound of crunching bacon is what consumers prefer".

"While there was much debate amongst our tasting panel on the smoked or unsmoked decision, everyone agreed that tough or chewy bacon is a turn off" he went on.

For the mathematically challenged, the formula for perfect is two or three back bacon rashers cooked under a pre heated oven grill for seven minutes at 240 C (475 F). The rashers should then be placed between two slices of the very freshest softest bread that are between 10 and 20 mm thick.

The formula itself translates as :- **N** = force in Newtons required to break the cooked bacon. **C** = Newtons required to break uncooked bacon. **Fb** = Functions of the Bacon type. **Cm** = Cooking Method. **Tc** = Cooking Time. **St** = Serving Temperature. **Fc** = Function of the Condiment and filling effect. **Ta** = Time or duration of application of sandwich assembly.

Aficionados of the bacon sandwich may feel that much important information is left out of this piece which appeared in the Daily Mail on April 10 th 2007. There is no mention of spread, nor the thickness of the bacon. In the authors view, butter is a must and the bacon should be thin, number 2 or 3 cut on the slicing machine. Furthermore, in our view, streaky back bacon provides a better result particularly if the crispy effect if sought. To crisp, the bacon must be left to dry in air. As for smoked or unsmoked, smoked is by far the most flavoursome but maple cured tops them all. There is also no mention of sauces, tomato or HP. Both are fine on sausages in our view, but personally, the very special flavour and feel of good bacon with either of these overpowering acid/sugar dressings is anathema.

No mention is made of what sort of beverage should accompany a good bacon sandwich either. The saltiness requires that a drink of some kind is enjoyed alongside. Probably tea for tea drinkers but my favourite is cold milk.

This is not the first time that scientists have calculated a formula for every day food tasks. Food scientist Dr Len Fisher of Bristol University paved the way by producing a formula for dunking a chocolate digestive in a cup of tea.

sandwiches
in space

A contraband beef sandwich was the subject of a US Congressional investigation and the first ever Congressional reprimand delivered to an astronaut.

The incident occurred on March 23rd, 1965 when Astronaut John Young smuggled a corned beef sandwich on rye aboard Gemini 3 to supplement the then unpalatable and untried space rations devised by NASA.

Young had purchased the sandwich from a delicatessen in Coca Beach, Florida but history does not relate how he smuggled it aboard or how 'old' it was at the time of consumption.

During the five-hour mission while orbiting the earth, Young offered the sandwich to mission mate Virgil I. Grissom. Grissom did not finish the sandwich because it was producing crumbs which in the weightless environment of a space craft, was problematic (I have nearly the same problem in my car).

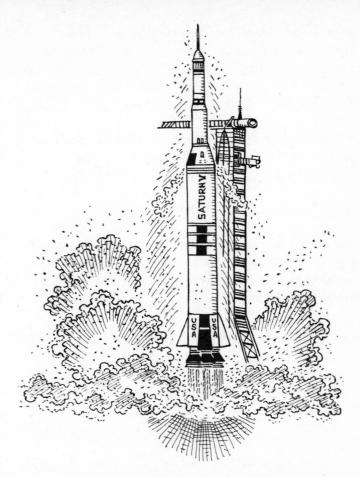

"Lunch? Sorry Huston we
thought you said Launch."

Grissom later described the meal as one of the 'highlights' of the flight. One of NASA's more colourful characters, he was killed in 1966 during a routine pre-flight test on Apollo 1 when fire broke out inside the capsule.

A KFC chicken sandwich was launched into space on board a high altitude World View Enterprises Stratollite weather balloon on June 29th 2017. Reaching 80,000 feet, the sandwich stayed aloft for nearly four days before returning to earth.

The advertising stunt was as much about the balloon company as it was about the sandwich and inclusion in this section of the Sandwich Companion is proof the mission was successful.

"... One small snack for man
One giant meal for mankind..."

sandwiches
in literature

"**Mr Bloom** *ate his strips of sandwich with relish of disgust, fresh clean bread, pungent mustard, the feety savour of greencheese*"
James Joyce: *'Ulysses'*

"**I will** eat a butterfly sandwich and wait till the shower is over ... "
Beatrix Potter: *'The Tale of Mr Jeremy Fisher'*

" ...**coldtongue***coldhambeefpickledgherkinssalad-frenchrollscresssandwichespottedmeatgingerbeerlem-onadesodawater...*"
Kenneth Grahame: *'The Wind in the Willows'*

"**Heads, heads**, *take care of your heads.. .*
Five children - Mother - tall
Lady eating sandwiches, forgot the arch - crash - knock - children look round - mother's head off - sandwich in her hand- no mouth to put it in - head of a family off - shocking, shocking!"
Charles Dickens: *'Pickwick Papers'*

"**Who're you** makin' sandwiches for?" he demanded.
His mother surveyed him sadly.
"I do wish you could keep clean for more than two minutes together, William," she said.
William smoothed back an obstreperous mop of hair with a grimy hand. "Yes," he agreed mechanically, "but who're you makin' sandwiches for?"
Richmal Crompton: 'Just William'

"**A naked** lunch is natural to us, we eat reality sandwiches. But allegories are so much lettuce. Don't hide the madness."
Allen Ginsberg: 'On William Burrough's work'

"**I did not know** I was excluding a revered sandwich-board man of the revolution and that somebody has put his worst and most famous poem in a glass-case at the British Museum - however if I had known it I would have excluded him just the same. He is all blood, dirt and sucked sugar stick."
W.B. Yeats: Referring to Wilfred Owen in a letter to Dorothy Wellesley.

"**He (Paddington)** rubbed his eyes and followed Judy and Jonathan up the beach to where Mrs Bird had layed out the sandwiches - ham, egg, and cheese for everyone else, and special marmalade ones for Paddington..."
Michael Bond: 'A Bear called Paddington'

Sandwiches in Politics

David Cameron revealed that he had once had the ham from a sandwich he was eating stolen by a seagull.

The then Prime Minister told a reporter from the Western Morning News that he had fallen victim to an attack from the skies. "I haven't felt particularly oppressed by seagulls. In my distant past I remember a seagull taking the ham out of a sandwich I was holding. But I haven't held that against the entire seagull population." He said.

Cameron told the story to the newapaper following reports that £250,000 had been committed in the budget to tackling the impact of "urban gulls".

Sandwiches in Crime

Alan Hunt, 36 (Sept 03 time of writing) was thrown into a police cell for eating half of a cheese sandwich belonging to PC Chris Briggs.

Jobless actor Hunt, was taking part in an identity parade for Dorset Police when, feeling hungry, he stole a lunch box and shared out the contents with fellow paraders. The lunch included an apple, a cake, a nectarine and a cheese sandwich.

PC Briggs was furious when he discovered what had happened and declined Hunt's offer to buy him a baguette in recompense.

£118.00 of court costs were run up along with hours of police officers time as Hunt was brought before East Dorset Magistrates and ordered to pay £25.00 costs but given a conditional discharge.

The Daily Express reported Hunts remarks after the hearing. " That was an expensive cheese sandwich. It wasn't even any good. I only ate half and it was bloody terrible. Theft was the last thing on my mind."

Prosecutor Tim O Sullivan told the court that Hunt's £10 fee for appearing on the parade was withheld.

Defence council Alison Brooking said that Hunt only did it because he was hungry.

Doorstep: Fond term for a thick sandwich...

record sandwiches

Biggest...
Marks and Spencer celebrated Sandwich week in 2000 by displaying the world's biggest sandwich, made by McVities. Weighing 400kg and measuring 7ft 9in it consisted of tuna, cucumber and mayonnaise between two massive slices of white bread. Ten people took five hours to make it!

Biggest sandwich catastrophe...
An attempt in Iran to beat the world record largest sandwich failed when the spectator crowd ate the sandwich before it could be measured.

Dignitaries from the Guinness Book of Records and organisers watched in despair as the 1.5 kilometre long sandwich began to disappear when the crowd surged forward and started guzzling the sandwich. Bizarrely the effort was organised in a city park in the centre of Tehran, Capital of Iran. 1,500 metres of bread was being stuffed with 700 Kilograms of Ostrich meat and 700 Kilograms of chicken watched by a large crowd who must have grown increasingly hungry at the sight. In despair, the organisers collected as much video footage of the event as they could and prevailed upon the officials from Guinness to analyse it and try to determine if the record had indeed been broken.

The existing largest sandwich recorded in the Guinness book of world records was achieved in Wild Woody's Chill and Grill in Roseville, Michigan, USA on March 17th 2005. The sandwich weighed 2,467.5 kilos. It contained 68 kg of mustard, 468.1 kg of corned beef, 117.9 kg of cheese, 240.4 kg of lettuce all enclosed in 1,618.4 kg of bread.

On balance, the Iranian effort looks as if it could have topped this but guarding 1.5 kilometres of sandwich from a hungry crowd had not been considered carefully enough in Tehran.

Most difficult... On 10th November, 2000, Rob Williams (USA) made a bologna, cheese and salad sandwich in 1 minute 57 seconds, using just his feet!

Most unusual... Wriggleys Spearmint Gum sandwich. Apparently, it lasts all lunch time and most of the afternoon too.

Most remote...16 year old Australian teenager Jade Hameister skied to the South Pole. She had already reached the north pole and skated across the Greenland ice cap. Quite a feat for someone so young. However misogynistic internet trolls taunted her with comments like " Hi Sweetie, make me a sandwich". Her response was to make a ham sandwich and post a picture of it at the south pole along with the remark. "Now ski for 37 days to the south pole and collect it".

Most appearances of the word "sandwich" in one book. The words Sandwich, sandwiches or sandwiched appear in the Essential Sandwich Companion which you are now holding, no fewer than 661 times which is thought to be a world record.

Most expensive...
The most expensive sandwich in the world was made by Philpotts sandwich shop in Manchester during the Manchester Food and Drink Festival in 1999. Priced at £170, with profits going to charity, the recipe (created by International Master Chef Tom Bridge) contained the following ingredients: 8oz of lobster tail meat; 8oz of smoked salmon marinated in champagne; a dozen smoked oysters; 2oz of beluga caviar; 14 oz of parma ham; two smoked chicken breasts; four large tablespoons of English mustard; four large tablespoons of mayonnaise; 12 spinach leaves and a dash of salt and pepper, washed down by a large helping of Dom Perignon champagne.
Ironically, a sample made up for an appearance on Granada Television's 'Granada Reports' was eventually given free to a local bag lady who must have felt exceptionally well rewarded for her day's labours.

None were sold but the sandwich achieved its public relations objectives.

Fastest...
The record for fastest 'bun' in the West goes to a team of bakers from Montana, USA who reclaimed the Guinness World Record in 1995.
They harvested and milled wheat from the field, then mixed, scaled, shaped and baked a loaf in just eight minutes and thirteen seconds.

Most money paid ...
The most money paid for a sandwich was in 2004 in America when somebody found that their toasted baguette had the image of the Virgin Mary on the crust. An anonymous buyer paid $28,000.00 for it.

The World record for eating 8 oz corned beef sandwiches is 20 in 10 minutes. This astonishing guzzle was achieved by No.1 competitive eater Joey Chestnut in 2012. He also allegedly holds the record for grilled cheese sandwich eating. 47 in 10 minutes.

The oldest known bread was baked 14,400 years ago in North East Jordan. Danish archaeologists announced this find in July 2018. The bread pre dates agriculture and is thought may have encouraged its producers to find a better way of producing the required grains other than foraging in the wild. The bread is praised by Professor Tobias Richter from Copenhagen University, as being of high quality and containing flour not just from cereal grains, but tubas too.

"There is hardly anything in the world which some man cannot make a little worse and sell a little cheaper and the people who buy on price only are this man's lawful prey"

John Ruskin

Sandwiches abroad

Essential phrases for sandwich lovers travelling to unusual places.

English: "Excuse me Sir/Madam but can you tell me where I can buy a decent sandwich around here?"

And now in the following languages: -

Afrikaans: Verskoon tog Meneer / Dame, maar kan u my dalk se waar ek 'n hier rond 'n lekker toebroodjie kan koop?

Arabic:

شتودندسن)ةقئلا ةري-طرش ءارش نمكنني يمكنكم ن أي يربرنخت نكن أن هل رجاءً، رجا ،
لائق (ق هنا جلوارا؟"

Basque: Barkatu jaun / anderea, non eros dezaket behar bezalako ogitarteko bat hemen inguruan?

Bengali

আমাকে ক্ষমা করবেন মহাশয় / মহাশয়া, অনুগ্রহ করে আপনি কি আমাকে বলতে পারেন আমি এখানে আশপোশে কোথা থেকে একটি ভাল স্যান্ডউইচ কিনিতে পারি

Cape Verdean Creole: "Kon lisensa Sinhor / Sinhora, Pur favor Nhu/Nha podi fla-m undi ki-m podi kunpra un sanduíxi dretu pa li?"

Chinese: "先生/女士，冒昧打扰一下，请问您能告诉我附近哪儿可以买到一个好吃的三明治吗？"

Dutch: "Sorry voor het storen, Mijnheer/Mevrouw, maar kan u mij alstublieft informeren waar ik hier in de buurt een deftig broodje kan kopen?

Pidgin English (West Africa): Oga / Madam, excuse me, Abeg you sabi where I fit buy sandwich wey good well well for dis area?

Esperanto: Pardonu min, sinjoro/sinjorino. Ĉu vi povus indiki al mi kie mi povas aĉeti akcepteblan sand-viĉon proksime de ĉi tie?

Finnish: "Anteeksi hyvä herra / hyvä rouva, mutta voisitteko kertoa minulle, mistä täältä saisi ostaa kunnon voileivän?"

French: « Excusez-moi Monsieur / Madame. Pourriez-vous me dire où je peux acheter un sandwich décent dans le quartier ?

German: "Entschuldigen Sie bitte mein Herr/meine Dame, können Sie mir sagen, wo ich hier in der Umgebung ein gutes belegtes Brot kaufen kann?"

Greek: Με συγχωρείτε, κύριε / κυρία, μπορείτε παρακαλώ να μου πείτε πού μπορώ να αγοράσω ένα καλό σάντουιτς εδώ κοντά;

Greenlandic: Utoqqatserpunga, qanittumi sumimita sandwichimik iluameersumik pisisinnaavunga?

Hebrew: השקבב הלוכי/לוכי תא/התא ,יתרבג יל יחלס / ינודא יל חלס
?הביבסב / רוזאב [גנלס] ילמרונ 'זיוודנס תונקל רשפא הפיא יל דיגהל

Igbo: (South Eastern Nigeria) (see this chapter 'Yaruba' for South Western Nigeria) Cheregodi Saar/ Ma, Biko inwere ike gwa m ebe m ga azuta ezigbo nri eji atagharonu na gburugburu ebe a?

Jamaican Patois: " Excuse mi sir/madam yuh cya tell mi weh mi cya buy a gud sandwich bi mi?"

Japanese:「すみません、この近くで、ちゃんとしたサンドイッチが買えるところを教えていただけませんか。」

Latin: Me excusa domine/domina, si vobis placet, potesne mihi narrare quo possim bonum pastillum fartum emi prope hunc locum?

Mandingo: "Ihakketu mbadi Keo / Muso, Dukare isi dula yitanna nooba janse sandwich diima sanno dame?"

Mauri: Tena koe, e Sir, Ka taea e koe te korero mai ki ahau te wahi e taea ai e au te hoko i te hanewiti pai i konei?

Oromo: Dhiifama Giifti/Obbo, maaloo naannoo kanaa saaduuchii gaarii eessaa bitachu akkan danda'u natti himu dandeessaa?

Pashto: "بخښنه غواړم مريم/ افطل ام ته واهيه زه
دلته نزدي ي وش هش کوم خاي اخيستلی شم؟"

Romany: Jeftisaren Rajo/Rajnie, šaj te vakeren mange kaj šaj kate khatende te ćinav khajek mišto sendviči?

Russian: (Cyrillic) Извините, подскажите, пожалуйста, где здесь поблизости можно купить нормальный сэндвич?

Russian: (Transcription) Izvinite, podskazhite pozhalusta, gde zdes' poblizosti mozhno kupit' normal'niy senvich?

Turkish: "Afedersiniz Bayım / Bayan, bu yakınlarda nereden iyi bir sandviç alabilirim söyleyebilir misiniz acaba?"

Urdu: "معاف کیجیے گا سر/میڈم، برائے مہربانی کیا آپ مجھے بتا سکتے ہیں، میں یہاں کہ میری اردو گرد کیا اچھا سینڈ وچ سٹور (یہاں خرید سکتے ہوں)؟"

Welsh: "Esgisodwch fi, fedrwch chi ddeud wrthai lle gai brynnu brechdan arbennig yn yr ardal?"

Vietnamese: "Phiền quý ông/quý bà có thể chỉ cho tôi biết chỗ mua sandwich ở quanh đây được không?"

Yoruba: (South western Nigeria. See this chapter 'Igbo' for south eastern Nigeria) Ẹgafara mi alagba / Iyaafin, Ẹjọwọ se ẹ le sọ ibi ti mo ti le ra onjẹ ipanu to dara ni itosi ibi?

Zulu: "Uxolo mnumzane/nkosazana, ngicela ukubuza. Ngingayitholaphi indawo edayisa ikota elimnandi eduzane?"

Best airport sandwich offer:- Schiphol (Amsterdam.)
Worst country for finding sandwiches:- Cuba.
Biggest sandwiches:- USA.
Smallest sandwiches:- New Zealand.
Worst sandwiches:- Spain.
Best sandwiches:- London UK.
Widest sandwich choice:- Sydney, Australia.

Shortest sandwich menu:- Havana, Republic of Cuba. The elegant stone collonaded National Hotel in central Havana is one of the most beautiful Spanish colonial buildings in the country. Its magnifiscent portals and gardens, fountains, swimming pools and peacocks are host to the great and the good who assemble in lavish splendour on the terrace to enjoy coffee, cocktails, cigars and sandwiches.

The sandwich offer is:- 1. Jamon (ham), 2. Queso (cheese) or 3. Jamon queso (Ham and cheese). That's it.

secrets of Super sandwich making

As with anything, you can make good sandwiches and bad ones. This is how to make good ones.

There are two overriding principles which all sandwich makers need to know before even thinking about making a sandwich.

First principle. It is the sandwich makers' first and absolute duty to exclude all kinds of undesirable elements which may be contained in a food used as a sandwich ingredient. Sandwiches are eaten blind while meals eaten from plates with a knife and fork allow the diner to inspect each mouthful and discard the bones or gristle nobody in their right mind wants to eat.

There really is nothing more horrible than an unexpected 'find' in a sandwich, and the mind plays awful tricks at this moment. For uncooked bacon becomes shredded fan belt and chicken bone anything from glass chard to Monty Python's famous 'Spring Surprise'*.

The unspeakable mouth feel of cartilage, sinew, skin or the 'wrong' kind of fat grips a sandwich eater with disgust and shatters their faith in the rest of the meal. A bad experience of this kind can induce Sandwich Aversion Disorder (SAD) for anything from a few hours up to a year.

An eater of sandwiches relies wholly on the diligence of the sandwich maker to ensure there are no unpleasant surprises. It is an invisible bond of trust which every sandwich consumer gives silently and willingly every time he or she bites into the unknown strata between two slices of bread. It is a trust that, once breached, cannot be mended. It is a duty of care to which every sandwich maker must be committed.

Significantly, Mrs Beeton in her famous 19th Century book of household management, rubs all her sandwich recipes through a fine sieve (AND cuts off the crusts before serving). This procedure will have ensured the unhindered integrity of her sandwiches but we should bear in mind that those who were eating them also probably had no teeth.

Second principle. Use same day baked good quality bread.

* *Spring Surprise* was the name of the smooth vanilla fondant cream chocolate which, once bitten into, triggered two powerful spring loaded bolts piercing both cheeks.
Monty Python sketch circa 1969.

✔ Always make sandwiches on a board, not a plate. If possible, bread should be hand sliced from the loaf - discarding the first slice, which may have been exposed to the air and become dry.

✔ Butter is best, but whichever spread you use, commence round the perimeter of the slice. The middle will take care of itself.

✔ For flavour, use ingredients that compliment each other and always remember to balance fat with acid - cheese and onion, ham and pickle, etc.

✔ Leaf salads can be added or omitted from practically any combination.

✘ Do not use flavours that fight with each other: for example, tomato and salmon. The former will overpower the latter.

✘ Do not use flavoured breads for they will undermine and fight with the flavour of the ingredients.

✔ Always remember to season with salt and pepper.

✔ Use mayonnaise as often as you want or any other agent such as yoghurt to bind and moisten your sandwich.

✘ When making sandwiches for yourself, never make two the same. You may be using ham, so make one plain but put mustard or tomato with the second. With cheese, make one with mayonnaise and the other with pickle or relish. Slake your hunger on the first and savour the excitement of the second.

✘ Don't squash the air out of your sandwich when cutting, or your ingredients when spreading. Air assists the flavour of both bread and ingredient.

✔ Use 'Reverse Crust Profiling' (RCP) (See Chapter A-Z of Sandwiches, 'RCP':) to make slices from an irregular shaped loaf match each other. Butter and use the reverse side of alternate slices.

✔ Always take your ingredients to the very edge of the bread and in some cases, allow them to protrude generously.

✘ Avoid 'pyramiding', the habit of piling and overlapping ingredients so that the most is in the middle while the extremities are thin. There is nothing worse than an 'empty corner' particularly if your bread is not up to scratch. Aim always to have an even thickness of ingredients from corner to corner.

✔If sandwiches are for eating later, shield the bread from moist ingredients such as tomato using lettuce or thick butter. This moisture barrier is vital if your sandwiches are to remain in prime condition. Better still, avoid the moist ingredients altogether. Wrap with traditional waxed paper, aluminium foil or in a polythene bag. Never use cloth, paper or clingfilm.

✔Always think about texture. Use lettuce or cucumber with cheese but think about potato crisps or tortilla chips with chicken or turkey, and crackling with pork.

✔'Minefields' are always exciting; a powerful dot of mustard or chilli sauce off centre so that even you won't know where it is.

✔Whether you prefer to cut into two or four triangles or rectangles, make sure you have cut right through. Use the knife blade to separate one half from the other by just enough to ensure a clean cut. There is nothing worse than pulling out one half of your sandwich and dragging to pieces the second half because of an incomplete cut.

X With ingredients, don't confuse quantity with quality. This occurs all the time in America. The ratio between bread and ingredients is critically important and too many sandwiches are ruined by too much (or too little) ingredient. Too much ingredient creates a sandwich your mouth can't get a top and bottom bite of and the whole thing collapses in your hands and over your trousers. Watch out for sandwiches requiring a vertical wooden skewer to hold them together, it portends a disappointing lunch and a dry cleaning bill!

X Eating sandwiches while driving a motor vehicle is dangerous and can result in a police prosecution. Attempting to eat a sandwich while driving a car with a manual gearbox is particularly dangerous. Turning right at a busy cross roads is impossible. With a hands-free (automatic) car, things are easier but it is still dangerous and should not be attempted.

Passengers on the other hand are subject to no such restrictions but should be mindful of their choice of ingredient. Avoid sandwiches full of 'bits', i.e. salad. Avoid all but the very softest and flattest of rolls to guard against the danger of squeezing ingredients out when biting.

Keep to modestly filled wedges of well-bound ingredients (not too loose) such as egg mayonnaise, chicken coronation or a tuna recipe. These sandwiches are easy to control leaving one hand free to hold a telephone, a drink, or indicate to the driver points of interest along the route. A mayonnaise covered slice of tomato slipping out of your sandwich and heading for your crotch is likely to spoil your trousers and your journey as well as your lunch. As with all food eaten off the knee, a large napkin to catch crumbs is recommended.

X Never cut buns, baguettes or rolls vertically to stuff ingredients in from the top. It looks attractive but makes hideous eating with mayonnaise requiring to be wiped from the nose after each bite. Sandwiches made in this way cruelly deny the eater of a crusty bite or the satisfying 'mouth feel' of your teeth passing through a friendly layer of bread before bursting into the ingredient strata.
(See Chapter 'A-Z of Sandwiches','VCB':)

Discussions about whether to cut a sandwich diagonally from corner to corner to make two triangles or 'east-west' to create two rectangles can lead to violence. The opposing arguments can be as fiercely contested as those about which way up a boiled egg should be approached.

Triangles. Easy to get a corner into your mouth BUT the pointed nature of the wedge can be unsupportive of ingredients (in a well-made sandwich in which the ingredients go right into the corners) which can fall out, especially if it is a well filled sandwich. And as you bite off the first corner that presents itself, what is happening at the other end? This could easily become a 'Banjo' situation (See chapter A-Z of sandwiches. 'Banjo sandwich':)

Rectangles. Very much the writer's personal preference.

Battery Sandwich: '..."the alternative being a buxom lady in a pinny with a loaf of bread and a slab of butter. .."

sandwich recipes

The following recipes make two rounds - (See chapter A-Z of sandwiches, 'Round':)
To make more sandwiches, simply multiply ingredients accordingly.

 denotes a sandwich suitable for vegetarians

Mozzarella, Cherry Tomatoes, Parma Ham, Rocket and Purple Basil

75g Buffalo mozzarella
6 cherry tomatoes
6 slices of Parma ham
6 sprigs of rocket
6 sprigs of purple basil
2 tablespoons mayonnaise

Grate the mozzarella into a mixing bowl. Mix in chopped slices of Parma ham and cherry tomatoes. Roughly tear the rocket and basil before adding to the bowl then mix in a tablespoon of mayonnaise.
Season well and spread generously.

*Pear, Crumbled Stilton and Watercress
Drizzled with Honey and Olive Oil Dressing*

1 ripe pear
75g crumbled stilton
A small handful of watercress

Honey and Olive Oil Dressing:

2 teaspoons lemon juice
2 teaspoons honey
2 teaspoons olive oil

Mix the olive oil, honey and lemon. Peel and slice the pear and arrange across bread. Add crumbled Stilton and scatter sprigs of watercress on top.

Season with freshly milled sal de mer and pepper. Using a teaspoon, drizzle the honey and olive oil over the watercress.

Chicken Breast, Caramelised Onions, and Crispy Bacon

120g roast chicken
1 small onion
25g crispy bacon
1 dessertspoon mayonnaise
1 clove garlic
1 desert spoon olive oil
1 teaspoon lemon juice
1 teaspoon sugar
1 teaspoon vinegar
1 teaspoon butter
salt, pepper

Slice peppers into thin strips and place on baking sheet. Sprinkle with chopped garlic, olive oil and lemon juice then place in the oven to roast. Roughly slice the onion and put into a pan with vinegar, sugar and butter and cook until soft and brown. Now add the chicken and roast peppers to the caramelised onion, add the bacon and stir in the mayonnaise. Season to taste. Serve in thick, soft bread.

Pastrami, Cream Cheese, Dill Cucumbers and a Mild Mustard Mayo

120g brisket pastrami
40g full fat cream cheese
1 pickled dill cucumber

Mild Mustard Mayo:

1 tablespoon mayonnaise
1 teaspoon salad cream
½ teaspoon English mustard
pinch of turmeric

Thinly slice the pastrami and cut into strips. Finely dice the dill cucumber. Mix both ingredients with the cream cheese in a bowl until the cream cheese softens. Spread on bread, bagel or baguette and follow with mustard mayonnaise and seasoning.

Cambazola (or Brie de Meaux) with Semi Dried Tomatoes, Mixed Leaves and Toasted Sunflower Seeds

120g Cambazola or Brie de Meaux
40g sun blushed or semi dried tomatoes
1 handful of mixed leaves
15g sunflower seeds

Slice the cheese and arrange across bread. Evenly space the semi dried tomatoes on top. Toss the sunflower seeds in a hot, dry pan until smoking and then sprinkle them over the other ingredients before adding the salad leaves. Mayonnaise optional. Most excellent in a crusty roll or baguette.

Chicken Breast with Melted Cheddar, Jalapenos and Chilli Mayo

120g shredded roast chicken
75g Cheddar cheese
2 jalapenos
1 handful tortilla chips

Chilli Mayonnaise:

2 tablespoons mayonnaise
a good splash of Tobasco
½ teaspoon chilli powder
squeeze of lemon
salt, pepper

Cover the bread with chicken. Finely chop the jalapenos and grate the cheddar. Mix both together in a bowl with the chilli mayonnaise.
Arrange mixture to cover the chicken completely and put under the grill. Top with crushed tortilla chips before adding the top slice of bread.

Roast Lamb, Crumbled Feta, Roasted Peppers in a Minted Mayo

120g shredded roast lamb
75g crumbled feta cheese
1 red pepper
1 clove of garlic
2 teaspoons extra virgin olive oil

Minted Mayonnaise:

2 tablespoons mayonnaise
a good splash of Tobasco
½ teaspoon chilli powder
squeeze of lemon
salt, pepper

Thinly slice the pepper and place on a baking sheet. Sprinkle with garlic and olive oil, season and place in a hot oven for 10 minutes.
When cooked, place in a mixing bowl together with the lamb and cheese: Finally, add the minted mayonnaise and stir. Season to taste.

Avocado, Cherry Tomatoes, Mixed Peppers and Red Onions in a Coriander Dressing

1 large ripe avocado, peeled
4 cherry tomatoes
1 red pepper
1 yellow pepper
1 small onion
1 teaspoon lemon juice
salt, pepper

Coriander Dressing:

2 tablespoons of extra virgin olive oil
1 teaspoon of horseradish sauce
a pinch of dried mixed herbs
1 clove of garlic
a dash of lemon juice
1 teaspoon wholegrain mustard
1 tablespoon vinegar
3 fresh coriander leaves.

Finely dice the peppers and onion. Roughly slice and chop the avocado into a mixing bowl. Add lemon juice and stir. Add the peppers, onion and tomatoes, mix and season with plenty of salt and pepper.

149

Mix up the dressing ingredients in a blender. Spread the avocado mixture across a well buttered slice of bread or baguette and drizzle generously with the dressing.

Cumberland Sausage, Crispy Bacon, Sauteed Onions and Cranberry Sauce

160g cooked Cumberland sausages
30g cooked smoked bacon
1 small onion
1 teaspoon butter
1 teaspoon cranberry sauce
1 tablespoon mayonnaise

Peel and roughly chop the onion before cooking on a medium heat with the butter and cranberry sauce. Stir frequently until clear. Allow to cool. Slice the sausages into small pieces and finely shop the smoked bacon before mixing both together. Add the cooled onion mix and stir in the mayonnaise. Use thick, white, well buttered bread.

Smoked Cheese, Roasted Peppers and Toasted Almonds in a Basil Mayo

100g smoked cheese
1 red pepper
1 yellow pepper
25g almonds
1 teaspoon butter
A few leaves of basil
1 teaspoon of extra virgin olive oil
1 clove of garlic
2 tablespoons mayonnaise

Thinly slice the peppers and sprinkle with olive oil, chopped garlic and seasoning. Bake in a medium hot oven for 10 minutes while browning the almonds in a pan. Grate the smoked cheese and mix in chopped basil leaves. Now add the peppers and almonds and mix all of them together. The mayonnaise can be either stirred into the mixture or spread on the top slice of bread, or eliminated altogether.

Hummus and Oven Roasted Vegetables

2 dessert spoon hummus
1 small red onion
1 yellow pepper
1 carrot
1 stalk of celery
2 baby corn
1 teaspoon wholegrain mustard
1 clove of garlic
1 tablespoon olive oil
1 teaspoon honey
salt, pepper

Roughly chop all the vegetables and place in a baking tin. Sprinkle with olive oil, chopped garlic and honey and toss until evenly coated. Cook for 40 minutes in a medium oven until tender. Spread the hummus thickly onto buttered bread. Top with the roasted vegetables and season to taste.

Cheddar and Mint Mustard Minefield

120g sliced Cheddar cheese
8 leaves of fresh garden mint
½ teaspoon fresh English mustard

Arrange cheese evenly across bread. Place two generous 'dots' of mustard at random (not so close as to risk both 'mines' detonating in the same bite). Place mint leaves on top, one in each quarter.

Surf 'n Turf with Marie Rose Sauce

80g cooked sirloin of beef, sliced
80g cooked prawns
squeeze of lemon juice
a handful of mixed leaves

Marie Rose Sauce:

2 tablespoons mayonnaise
1 teaspoon tomato sauce
a dash of Worcester Sauce
1 teaspoon horseradishs auce

Slice the beef into thin strips and add the prawns and
lemon juice with a couple of turns each of salt and
pepper. Fold in the Marie Rose Sauce and spread onto
well buttered bread. Top with mixed leaves.
Alternatively add the Marie Rose sauce separately
onto the top or bottom slice of bread.

Cheese and Onion

120g sliced, ripe, mature farmhouse Cheddar cheese
1 Spanish onion
1 tablespoon mayonnaise (optional)

Dice the onion. Arrange the Cheddar cheese to cover the bread then spread the mayonnaise across it. Now sprinkle onion on top to taste. Onion will stick to the mayonnaise. Thick slices of floppy crusty farmhouse loaf add to the pleasure.

Brie and Oven Baked Tomato

2 beef tomatoes
90g ripe brie or brie de Meaux
1 small red onion
2 basil leaves
2 teaspoons xtra virgin olive oil

Cut tops off the tomatoes and remove core, flesh and seeds. Roughly chop brie, onions and basil and mix together. Stuff mixture into tomato shells and place on a baking tray. Cook in a medium oven for 10 minutes until soft. Now squash between two cold plates until roughly sandwich sized and allow to cool. Place on bread and season before adding mixed leaf salad. Drizzle with olive oil.

Egg Mayonnaise / Egg and anchovies/Egg and bacon/Egg and Crispy Bacon/Egg and Smoked Salmon/ Egg and Flaked Smoked Haddock.

IMPORTANT DON'T SKIP THIS PAGE.

This is a stunning sandwich often spoiled or overlooked by eager sandwich makers in a hurry.

Egg is one of the humblest commonest sandwich ingredients in the western world.

But it can be dull, dry and awful or wildly exciting for want of a couple of usually missed ingredients.

There are many delicious variations in texture and content that I will come to later. But first read my secrets for the best egg mayonnaise sandwiches your friends will ever have tasted.

6 hard boiled eggs
Mayonnaise (Hellmann's is best)
Very very finely chopped onion
Finely chopped celery
Dijon or English mustard
Lemon juice
Salt
Pepper

Now check for texture. Your eggs may have been large or small! You may wish your egg mayonnaise to be moist or dry! Moist is good but NOT sloppy. Notice how the finely chopped celery is giving a crunchy texture, there may not be enough so add more. Notice how the finely chopped onion has greatly enhanced the flavour.... you may want to use less on a future occasion or add more as the case may be. But crucially, notice how the lemon juice, although not discernible as such, has brought the flavour out in spades. When this sandwich is made well, eaters cannot stop.

For this sandwich, I need to talk about bread. You can choose almost any bread you like providing it is fresh. But be aware that a moist ingredient in a stiff, perhaps crusty roll is likely to produce squeeze and, as Sir Clement Freud remarked to me once, "could necessitate a special arrangement with the people from Sketchley's".

One can now swing between extremes. Thick dryer mixture in wholemeal doorsteps, or a thin spread between thin white sliced bread with the crusts cut off.... cut into fingers. (See chapter A-Z of Sandwiches. 'Finger Sandwiches':)

Variations are limited only by your imagination. Cress or watercress in small or large quantities, always finely chopped.

Finely chopped parsley large or small leaf. A sprinkling of almost any herb you wish to choose.

Enhance the colour of your mixture with turmeric if you like. Alter the mixture by excluding 25% of your albumen (egg white) thus upping the concentration of yolk.

Be aware that over time, your mixture will tend to become dryer as the mayonnaise is absorbed into the yolks of your eggs. If kept overnight, one can easily add more mayonnaise the following morning to refresh the mixture.

Egg Mayonnaise and Anchovies

A simple but devastatingly effective flavour. Simply dot pieces of chopped anchovy across the base layer of egg before adding the top slice of bread. The salt, as mentioned before, adds enormously to the flavour of the egg mixture and the anchovies fight their own corner.

Egg Mayonnaise and Celery.

Chop a greater quantity of celery, and not as finely as with the standard egg mixture and throw across the base layer of egg. Healthy and crunchy.

Egg Mayonnaise and Smoked Salmon.

The smoked salmon can be chopped and mixed into the mixture, but a more even distribution will be achieved by adding the chopped smoked salmon on top of the base layer of egg. Some extra ground black pepper and even a small further squeeze of lemon juice. For this sandwich, your top slice of bread needs to be very well buttered to create a moisture barrier (and more flavour) and prevent the lemon juice making the bread soggy.

Egg Mayonnaise and Bacon.

The writers view is that bacon should never be introduced to a sandwich unless it is easily bitten through. There is nothing worse than an elastic silicon rubber-like rasher or tough over thick slice of bacon that requires the eater to grip the sandwich tightly and pull it away from the mouth while the teeth hang on for dear life. One is now hoping for a swift severing of this awkward ingredient which has already stolen the joy of the sandwich. It never comes. Either the hand grip must be loosened to allow the rasher to slide out from inside the sandwich, usually bringing with it various refugee ingredients, or the teeth must relinquish their hold so that hands may be used to hold the bacon directly while the teeth hack away.

None of it is satisfactory. There are two answers.

First answer. ALWAYS cut bacon into small pieces and distribute evenly over the sandwich, whatever the other ingredients may be.

Second answer (the writers preferred option). Use CRISPY bacon.
The taste of crispy bacon, and I mean really crispy bacon is a great pleasure. It enhances whatever other ingredients you choose, it never needs manual assistance, it adds crunch and in the case of egg mayonnaise, salt too.

Egg and Flaked Smoked Haddock.

A truly luxurious sandwich. Simply flake the poached smoked haddock over the base layer of egg mayonnaise and season with black pepper.

Avocado and crispy Bacon.

I used to refer to this sandwich as The King Sandwich and once had the honour of serving it to John Montague the Eleventh Earl of Sandwich himself at my home in Wales. His comment in the visitor's book on that occasion was "Sandwiches to die for".

Ripe avocado. Size 14 is about the best but bigger or smaller doesn't matter.
Crispy bacon.
Black pepper.
Mayonnaise.
Cut the avocado in half.

Peel one half per round of sandwiches using a small knife trying if possible to remove the skin without disturbing the surface of the avocado. This technique improves with practice. Hold the half avocado in the left hand, cut surface downwards and firmly put your forefinger in the hole where the stone once was. This gives you control and it is easy to put your blade just under an edge and raise a small flap of skin. With the thumb of your right hand holding the flap of peel to the blade, roll your hand back drawing the skin off. Two or three such movements should do the trick with a properly ripe avocado. In the case of hard skinned avocados, use a spoon or spatula to scoop the flesh from the skin.
The best colour and flavour of an avocado is in the flesh immediately below the skin so a good peeling technique improves all aspects of the sandwich as well as reducing waste.
Now place the peeled half avocado down on a chopping board, cut surface downwards and slice into as many thin slices as you like.

You can now fan out the slices and with a deft movement of the knife underneath at 90 degrees to your slices and with a hand on top, lift the entire fan and place it on the bottom buttered slice of bread. Use the knife or spatula to arrange the slices so as to cover as much of the bread as you can and then sprinkle broken up bits of bacon on top. Don't forget the black pepper. Salt is not necessary since the bacon provides this.

Personally, mayonnaise adds to the pleasure as well as giving the bacon bits something to adhere to.

Cream Cheese and Anchovies or Celery.

Both of these are delicious. Use full fat cream cheese. You can let the cream cheese down by mixing in some full fat milk which bulks up the ingredient layer and gives you a deeper bed into which you press either the anchovy pieces or the chopped celery. If making a large number of sandwiches, this also becomes an easier mixture to spread.

Season well and add lettuce if you wish

Feta Chilli Minefield with Julienne of Spring Onion, Flat Leaf Parsley and White Seedless Grapes

120g crumbled feta cheese
1 small red chilli
1 large spring onion
A few flat leaf parsley leaves
40g seedless green grapes cut lengthways
2 tablespoons mayonnaise or natural yoghurt

Shred or cut the spring onion into long, thin strips and chop the flat leaf parsley. Dissect the chilli and remove seeds then cut 6 rings - each about the size of a 5p. Thoroughly mix all the ingredients together in a bowl. Arrange on floppy white bread and press down top slice firmly.

further reading

'The Biggest Sandwich Ever'
Rita Gelman. Scholastic Inc.

'The Giant Jam Sandwich'
John Vernon Lord. Econ-Clad Books

'The Best Peanut Butter Sandwich in the Whole World'
Katherine Helmer. Firefly

'Sam's Sandwich'
Pelham, D. Dutton

'Bogart's Sandwich'
Riley, M. Park West

The Art of the Knuckle Sandwich
By Ricky Hansen

'Tunafish Sandwiches'
Hand Zandler. Random House

**'The Guide to Britain's Best Sandwich Bars'
available direct from the BSA at
www.sandwich.org.uk**
Trade Publications Ltd

**'Yes, but can the steam engine do this? -
Complete Prose'**
Woody Allen. Picador

**'The Top 136 UK Sandwich Makers
Companies'**
Plimsoll Publishing

'The Voyages of James Cook'
Edited by J.C. Beaglehole

**'The Endeavour Journals of Sir Joseph
Banks'**
Edited by J.C. Beaglehole

'The British Sandwich Association Sandwich Industry Review'
Taylor Nelson Sofres

International Master Chef Tom Bridge's book about sandwiches, which failed to make the shelves before this one, but will undoubtedly be a more sensible read!

**'The Pheasant Cook -
Ninety Seven Ways to Present a Bird'***
Tina Dennis and Rosamond Cardigan. *Crowood Press*

*Editor's note:
No mention of sandwiches, but Rodger McPhail's cover illustration of a whole pheasant between two slices of bread is exquisite!

I think it's Tracey Emin's unmade sandwich.